DISCIPLESHIP

LESSONS FOR THE CHRISTIAN LIFE

THOMAS F. LEAKE

KRESS
BIBLICAL
RESOURCES

Discipleship
Discipleship Lessons for the Christian Life
Copyright © 2016, © 2019, © 2020 by Thomas F. Leake

Published by Kress Biblical Resources
www.kressbiblical.com

ISBN 13: 978-1-934952-59-7

Printed in the United States of America

CONTENTS

STUDY 4
Focusing & Fruitfulness

STUDY 5
Failure & Forgiveness

STUDY 6
Fortifying for Spiritual Warfare

STUDY 7
Felicity (Joy), Forbearance,
Future Hope & Faithfulness

STUDY

1

FOUNDATIONS & FAITH

LESSONS 1-4

THE LORDSHIP OF JESUS CHRIST

Since the Scriptures clearly teach that Jesus is Lord, each of us must make sure we have personally accepted Jesus as the Lord of our lives.

Scriptural Teaching

1 CORINTHIANS 1:2 "To the church of God which is at Corinth, to those who have been sanctified in Christ Jesus, saints by calling, with all who in every place call on the name of our Lord Jesus Christ, their Lord and ours"

What makes someone a Christian? How do you know if you are a Christian? Are you a Christian because you have been baptized and attend church? Is someone a Christian by merely making a profession of faith in Jesus as Savior? Is someone saved simply by accepting certain facts about Jesus—that He died for our sins and was raised from the dead? These are foundational questions that should be addressed by each person wanting to make sure his or her relationship with God is right.

The Philippian jailor in ACTS 16:30–31 desperately asked the apostle Paul and his missionary traveling companion Silas, *"Sirs, what must I do to be saved?"* That is the right question to ask. This man earnestly wanted to know how to become a Christian and escape God's holy judgment. He was fearful of what would happen to him after he died. Fortunately for us, Paul and Silas gave him a direct and clear answer, *"Believe in the Lord Jesus, and you will be saved."* What a wonderful and simple promise! Faith in Jesus as Lord is what saves people and makes them Christians. Jesus must be believed in as one's personal "Lord."

What, then, does it mean to believe in the Lord Jesus? The Bible teaches that faith in Jesus must go beyond a mere profession of faith from the lips or even an intellectual agreement about certain facts concerning Jesus. Many people in the modern world believe certain facts about Jesus and then say they are Christians. That is not enough to be a true Christian. In his greeting to the Corinthian church, written above, the apostle Paul wrote that Christians are members of a group of people throughout the world who *"in every place call on the name of our Lord Jesus Christ."* To "call upon the name" of someone meant to invoke that person's help, abilities, and authority. To call upon "our Lord Jesus Christ" adds weight and definition to our calling. The Greek term for "Lord" used here and throughout the New Testament is *kurios*, which essentially means "a master or a sovereign." A "lord" was someone who had power, authority, and position.

So, Christians are those who call upon Jesus as their master and God. In other words, they acknowledge His authority and right to rule their lives. Christians call upon Jesus as "Lord" because that is His identity. He is not only a Savior. He is the Lord Jesus Christ. ROMANS 10:13 links salvation with our belief in Jesus' lordship this way: *"WHOEVER WILL CALL ON THE NAME OF THE LORD WILL BE SAVED."*

In the first century Roman world, to call Jesus "Lord" was to assert that Caesar was not the highest authority. Instead, Christ was the true Lord, Emperor, and King. The ancient Christians gave their highest loyalty not to the state but to Christ. Today, when we call upon Jesus as our Lord, we recognize His sovereign deity and right to rule our lives. As in the first century, Jesus must be the Lord of every believer today. He was Paul's Lord. He was the Corinthian's Lord. He was the Lord of every Christian in every place where they gathered for worship. He must also be our Lord.

Belief in the lordship of Christ is required of all believers. Contrary to some popular teaching, the Bible knows no such thing as a Christian who wants Jesus to save him from sins but rejects the rule of Jesus in his life. While it is true that none of us obey Jesus perfectly, or even as consistently as we wish, all true believers will submit their hearts to Christ's authority and grow in their obedience to His lordship over time. It is not the perfection of one's submission that marks him as a Christian, but the direction of that submission. From the day he believes in Jesus, that belief is a humble, submissive belief in his Lord and Savior—Jesus Christ.

1 CORINTHIANS 12:3 *"Therefore I make known to you that no one speaking by the Spirit of God says, 'Jesus is accursed'; and no one can say, 'Jesus is Lord,' except by the Holy Spirit."* This verse written by Paul adds to our understanding about the lordship of Jesus Christ. It lets us know that the Spirit of God is the One who motivates the human confession "Jesus is Lord." Some people may say the words without meaning, but no one can honestly confess that truth except by the Holy Spirit.

"Jesus is Lord" means that the human Jesus who walked on this earth is also the Divine Master of heaven. It is a confession that recognizes Jesus was not merely a man. He was the God-Man. As we already saw, confessing Jesus as Lord is necessary for every true believer. ROMANS 10:9 teaches, *"that if you will confess Jesus as Lord and believe in your heart that God raised Him from the dead you will be saved."*

So "Jesus is Lord" is the founding confession of the faith motivated by the Holy Spirit. If you do not confess Jesus as your Lord, you remain unsaved and are currently headed to judgment, even if you claim to be a Christian. That is because if Jesus is not your Lord, you are still in rebellion toward Christ's authority. 1 TIMOTHY 6:15 declares about Jesus, *"He who is the blessed and only sovereign, the King of kings and Lord of lords."* Each true believer, then, is willingly subject to the lordship of Jesus and promotes faith in Jesus as Lord. Just as Paul wrote in 2 CORINTHIANS 4:5, *"we do not preach ourselves but Christ Jesus as Lord."*

MATTHEW 7:21 *"Not everyone who says to Me, 'Lord, Lord,' will enter the kingdom of heaven, but he who does the will of My Father who is in heaven will enter."* This verse teaches us that there will be many people who call Jesus "Lord" but do not really mean it. Their profession of Jesus as Lord is discredited by their disobedience. Actions speak louder than words. So they will never make it into God's kingdom because they are not true believers. They are people who know of Jesus' authority and give lip service to it, but do not truly bow in obedience to Him.

Therefore it is not the one who merely declares that "Jesus is Lord" who is saved and gets into heaven, but the one who proves his profession of faith by doing the will of the Father. Doing God's will as revealed in the teachings of Jesus is the necessary mark, evidence, or sign that God has genuinely changed a sinner and saved him.

Jesus exposed people's inconsistent confessions in LUKE 6:46 when He asked, *"Why do you call me 'Lord, Lord, and do not do the things I say?"* Obeying Jesus does not save anyone. Yet, obeying Jesus is the necessary evidence we have truly believed in Him as Lord. Saying, "Lord, Lord" accomplishes nothing. Obeying the word of God is what God desires as the fruit of faith.

At the judgment, Jesus will reject many people who claim to know Him with these tragic words, *"Depart from me you who practice lawlessness!"*

Discussion & Application

1. What does it mean to confess Jesus as your Lord?

_____

_____

_____

_____

2. Have you confessed Jesus as your Lord, and do you see evidence of obedience in your life toward Jesus?

_____

_____

_____

_____

3. What are some ways you see people profess Christ as Lord yet do not demonstrate Him to be their Lord?

_____

_____

_____

_____

4. How can a believer consciously grow in the application of the lordship of Jesus?

_____

_____

_____

_____

5. In what ways would you desire to grow in your responsiveness to your Lord? Be specific!

_____

_____

_____

_____

Key Terms/Phrases

Kurios = the Greek term meaning 'lord' or 'master'

Profession of faith = what one claims to believe

Authority = the right and power to command others

Obedience = doing what one is told; the right response to the lordship of Jesus

Belief = a synonym for faith; belief results in obedience in the life of the believer

"Jesus is Lord" = founding confession of faith, which, if genuine, results in the confessing person's salvation

Further Exploration

Acts 2:21; 4:12; 20:24; Romans 13:14; Philippians 3:20; Colossians 3:17; Revelation 22:21

Suggested Memory Verse

ROMANS 10:9 *"that if you confess with your mouth Jesus as Lord, and believe in your heart that God raised Him from the dead, you will be saved."*

2

BELIEVING THE
TRUE GOSPEL

Since there are many different messages or
"gospels" being wrongly promoted as the
Christian message, believers should be confident
they know and accept the true, original gospel of
Jesus and then spread it to others.

Scriptural Teaching

MARK 16:15 *"Go into all the world and preach the gospel to all creation."*

What is the gospel we are to preach and believe? Have you believed it? Can you articulate it well to others? Can you distinguish it from false "gospels?" ROMANS 1:1 informs us the apostle Paul's life was *"set apart for the gospel of God."* Gospel, *euangelion* in Greek, means "good news" or "glad tidings." "The gospel of God" means the good news finding its source in God. In other words, it is God's good news to the world about salvation through His Son, Jesus. The disciples of Jesus went out and preached the gospel everywhere, ACTS 8:25,40; 14:7,15.

8

ROMANS 1:16 *"For I am not ashamed of the gospel, for it is the power of God to salvation for all who believe."* The true gospel expresses God's power in bringing men and women to salvation. It is something we are never to be ashamed to preach or teach. It will save anyone who believes. Christians should love the gospel of God and promote it.

GALATIANS 1:6–7 *"I am amazed that you are so quickly deserting Him who called you by the grace of Christ, for a different gospel; which is really not another; only there are some who are disturbing you and want to distort the gospel of Christ."* The apostle Paul knew that anyone who distorted or changed the true gospel of grace was not from God and was condemned. Therefore we must make sure we believe and preach the true gospel and reject all false gospels (which are really not gospels at all)!

2 CORINTHIANS 11:4 *"For if one comes and preaches another Jesus whom we have not preached, ... or a different gospel which you have not accepted, you bear this beautifully."* Paul rebuked the Corinthian church for not having discernment to distinguish the true gospel from false ones. They tolerated false gospels in their church. However, any Christian who tolerated false gospels was sinning and deserved Paul's rebuke. We certainly should not be known as Christians who accept or tolerate false gospels. That would not express loyalty to the true gospel.

I CORINTHIANS 15:1–5 *"Now I make known to you, brethren, the gospel which I preached to you, which also you received, in which also you stand, by which also you are saved, ... that Christ died for our sins according to the Scriptures, and that He was buried, and that He was raised on the third day according to the Scriptures, and that He appeared ...."* Here we read Paul's clear grasp of the Christian gospel. He teaches the gospel by revealing its four essential components.

Component # 1: Christ's Death

Jesus Christ, the Son of God, in His humanity died—literally and violently on a cruel, Roman cross. That is NOT the good news. This verse teaches that the good news is that Christ died "for sins." That means He died as a sacrifice to pay the penalty for our sins. He was punished for the sins for which we should have suffered. Since the consequence of sin for humanity is death (ROM. 6:23)—both physical death and ultimately eternal death in hell—Jesus died for us so we would not have to suffer eternal destruction. Notice that Jesus did not die for His own sins, since He had none (2 COR. 5:21). Jesus did not die merely to set a good example for us. Jesus died to pay for our sinful, rebellious, immoral, proud, selfish deeds. In one act of great grace and mercy, He suffered and died in our place! And He did it *"according to the Scriptures."* That means that when Christ died, He died to fulfill predictive prophecy and to carry out God's plan (LK. 24:45–47). It is all according to the written plan of God in Scripture to save us from our sins.

Component #2: Christ's Burial

You may wonder, "Why is the burial of Jesus part of the gospel? Do I really need to tell people about that?" Yes! All four of the gospel writers (Matthew, Mark, Luke, & John) give careful and explicit detail to the historical burial of Jesus of Nazareth. They record who took the body of Jesus down from the cross, who prepared it, where it was laid, what spices they put on the body, the cloth they wrapped around Him, even who stood guard at the tomb. These details are not incidental. The burial is an important part of the gospel a person is to believe, for it shows that Jesus was truly human and truly died. Jesus' death is a true event in human history.

The burial is an important proof of that death!

Component #3: Christ's Resurrection

The verb "raised" (used here in the perfect tense) stresses that Jesus was risen and stands risen to this day. It indicates an action done in the past with ongoing, present results. The same one who died is the same one who was buried, is the one who was raised, and is alive from the dead today; thus, Jesus is able to give life to any who believe in Him. He was raised on the third day to show that the historic prediction of His resurrection came true just as He said (MATT. 17:23). Dr. John MacArthur writes of the importance of the resurrection, "A follower of Buddha writes of that religious leader, 'When Buddha died it was with the utter passing away in which nothing whatever remains.' Mohammed died at Medina on June 8, 632, at the age of 61, and his tomb there is visited yearly by tens of thousands of Muslims. They come to mourn his death, not celebrate his resurrection. Yet the church of Jesus Christ, not just on Easter Sunday but at every service of baptism by immersion, celebrates the victory of her Lord over death and the grave." Again, the resurrection was all according to the plan of predictive prophecy just as Scripture foretold.

Component #4: Christ's Appearances

Just as the burial confirmed the death of Jesus, the multiple and varied appearances of Jesus to His disciples over 40 days with hundreds of eyewitnesses confirmed His resurrection as a fact of history. This provided people with hope of victory over death. This fourth component demonstrates that God has completed His work of salvation through His risen Son. God has demonstrated the victory of Jesus over man's greatest enemy—death. The work of saving us is accomplished. No other works of man is needed or even accepted by God. The way is Jesus Christ's finished work. This is the gospel of God, and it is truly good news!

Discussion & Application

1. Why do we need to believe all four components of the gospel of Jesus? How is each one essential?

_____

_____

_____

2. What is left for us to do after Jesus accomplished His death, burial, and resurrection?

_____

_____

_____

3. Why is the death & resurrection of Jesus good news? What would have happened to us if Christ had not accomplished this work?

_____

_____

_____

_____

4. Have you been articulating this specific and true gospel to others when you witness? How can you improve in your presentation?

_____

_____

_____

_____

Key Terms/Phrases

Gospel = the good news telling about Jesus as Savior

Salvation = deliverance and rescue from the coming wrath of God

Resurrection = bodily and physically being raised to life after clinical death

Predictive Prophecy = words from God in the Bible which accurately predict the future

Further Exploration

1 Corinthians 9:23; Galatians 1:11; Ephesians 1:13; 2:8–9; John 3:16–17; Colossians 1:23; 2 Timothy 1:10; 2:8

Suggested Memory Verse

1 CORINTHIANS 15:3–5 *"For I delivered to you as of first importance what I also received, that Christ died for our sins according to the Scriptures, and that He was buried, and that He was raised on the third day according to the Scriptures, and that He appeared ...."*

FAITH:
LESSON

3

SAVED BY GRACE
THROUGH FAITH

We are saved from sin and eternal punishment by
personal faith in Jesus Christ because salvation is a gift
of God's grace. The only way God's unmerited favor
can be received is by faith apart from human works.
Faith expresses the opposite of confidence in self-works.

Scriptural Teaching

EPHESIANS 2:8–9 *"For by grace you have been saved through
faith; and that not of yourselves, it is the gift of God; not as
a result of works, so that no one may boast."*

Here the word "grace," *charis*, in the original Greek, means
"unmerited favor." In usual human situations, favor with someone comes due to his merit or character; not so with grace.
Grace is unearned, undeserved, and unmerited. Grace cannot
be earned because we are all sinners. Sinners cannot earn anything from God except displeasure and judgment. Being res-
cued from God's judgment is by grace not by human religious
achievement or ethical works of any degree or kind. Take note

of the clear parallelism in these two verses: *By grace you are saved through faith/that not of yourselves; it is the gift of God/ not of works.* Clearly grace is a priceless gift to be humbly and thankfully received, never a reward for good works to be earned.

ROMANS 4:4–5 explains grace this way: *"Now to the one who works, his wage is not reckoned as a favor, but as what is due."* In other words, you do not say, "Thank you" when you get your paycheck from your workplace. It is not an undeserved gift. You earned it with your hard work, and you deserve it! *"But to the one who does NOT WORK, but BELIEVES in Him who justifies the ungodly, his faith is reckoned as righteousness."* Being justified by God, means to be pronounced innocent of all charges against you—as if in a court of law. So, with God as the judge, you do not, and in fact cannot, work for salvation, because no one can make himself innocent after breaking God's laws. Righteous innocence has to be given to you complete and entire as one undeserving of it! That is what it means to be saved by grace through faith.

So, if someone says something like, "I am hoping to get to heaven and avoid God's judgment because I have been a good person," that person obviously does NOT yet believe in the grace of God. He or she still hopes to get into heaven by human deeds or merit. Maybe the person thinks his church attendance, keeping the Ten Commandments, participation in the sacraments, or helping his neighbor will make it more likely he will go to heaven. However, like oil and water, grace and human works do not mix. Jesus came to save sinners, and we are all sinners. ROMANS 11:6 declares, *"but if it is by grace, it is no longer on the basis of works, otherwise grace is no longer grace."* What could be clearer! Salvation is all of grace, none of works. A gift paid for or earned by the recipient is no longer a gift.

If people could earn their way out of God's judgment and into heaven, they might have something to boast about, but EPHESIANS 2:9 emphasizes that we were saved by grace *"so that no one should boast."* Do people really boast before God? Yes, but some boasts are subtle like: "I have lived a pretty good life;" "I haven't done anything really bad;" "God knows I did my best." God hates all human boasting, for it ruins His wondrous display of His marvelous grace. To God, human pride is like a trash heap in a picturesque forest or an oil spill in beautiful tropical waters. God will not stand for any human boasting in salvation because it destroys the beauty of His grace. ROMANS 3:27 asserts that with God all human "boasting is excluded." The only one who gets to boast is God. God saves us by grace and exclaims, "Look! See what I have done, and marvel at My grand display of grace!"

What is the place of our faith, then, if we are saved entirely by God's grace? Faith in Jesus and His work of salvation is required for salvation, but not even our faith in Jesus earns for us salvation. Faith is only the instrument or means by which grace comes to us. In fact, salvation will not come to us without faith because faith is self-emptying. Faith is not a work we do or something self-manufactured. Faith no more earns us our salvation than a drowning person earns his rescue by desperately grabbing hold of a lifesaver thrown from a boat. Saving faith trusts completely in what Jesus did to save us, not what we do to help Him save us. To have faith in Jesus means to put confidence in Him and what He did on the cross. It is faith in Him and His resurrection, not trust in our good deeds or ourselves. Faith in Jesus is empty of self-righteousness and full of Christ-confidence. So, we are saved by grace through faith, and none of that is of ourselves.

EPHESIANS 2:10 *"For we are His workmanship, created in Christ Jesus for good works, which God prepared beforehand so that we would walk in them."* If we are saved by grace through faith, then why would we choose to do good works? What is the place of good deeds? According to this verse believers are God's workmanship. God is the craftsman! He does the good work of remaking us by His grace. When He gives us grace through the instrument of faith, then we are His new created product. We are His workmanship! So, all our truly good works come after God reworks us, not before our salvation. Good works are not the cause of our salvation; they are the result of God changing us. Think of it this way: Faith is the engine; good works are the caboose. Good works flow from our faith, but they are never a substitute for faith. So-called good works done before we believed are not truly good in God's sight, for they were done unto self-glory, not the glory of Christ.

Discussion & Application

1. Why does salvation have to be by grace and not by any works at all?

_____

_____

_____

_____

_____

2. Why can grace only be received by faith and not any other way?

_____

_____

_____

_____

_____

3. What is the relationship between faith and good works?

_____

_____

_____

_____

_____

Key Terms/Phrases

Grace = unmerited favor with God; the opposite of earned favor

Good works = good deeds humans do which do not save a person but follow after salvation

Justify = to pronounce innocent of guilt; justification with God is by faith alone in Christ alone

Righteousness = living rightly or correctly; also the demands of God's moral law; believers get righteousness as a gift of grace

Self-righteousness = the wrong thought that a person can attain his own good standing with God by his own practice of righteous living

Further Exploration

John 1:16; Acts 15:9; 18:27; 20:24; Romans 3:23–28; 4:16; 5:1f; 9:30; 11:6; 2 Corinthians 8:9; Galatians 3:22; Titus 3:7

Suggested Memory Verse

EPHESIANS 2:8–9 *"For by grace you have been saved through faith; and that not of yourselves, it is the gift of God; not as a result of works, so that no one may boast."*

4

GROWING IN FAITH THROUGH THE WORD OF GOD

After we are saved by grace, God continues to strengthen our faith through His word, so that we can experience His grace more deeply.

Scriptural Teaching

1 PETER 2:2 "Like newborn babes, long for the pure milk of the word that by it you may grow in respect to salvation."

The apostle Peter urges Christians to long for the pure milk of God's word. He previously wrote in chapter 1:23 that the word of God was living and abiding. He also wrote that the word was the gospel that was preached to them. Now he exhorts them to take that same word into their lives in greater amounts so they will grow in their new life in Christ. That is what you need to do, now that you are saved through faith in Jesus as Lord.

The noun for "word" here is *logikon* in Greek. It indicates that the word is spiritual, even logical nutrition for our souls. That is how the word of God feeds us—by giving our minds wonderful, rational truth about Christ to absorb into our being. In MATTHEW 4:4 Jesus quoted the Old Testament, "*MAN SHALL NOT LIVE ON BREAD ALONE, BUT ON EVERY WORD THAT PROCEEDS OUT OF THE MOUTH OF GOD.*" See how important the word of God is to our spiritual growth! The word of God produces the new birth in us, and it feeds and nourishes our souls to produce growth in faith. We live by the word of God.

Notice how Peter describes the word as "*the pure milk of the word.*" This adjective "pure" means "without guile or deceit." When applied to food it had the idea of purity of substance, as with pure wine or pure wheat. Purity exists when there is nothing else mixed with the food substance. It is the real stuff! Applied to God's word, it means there is nothing deceitful in the Bible. It speaks the pure truth to our souls. It is not empty philosophy without nutritional value! It is not false religion which poisons the soul. It is not unreliable myth or unworkable truth. The Bible is pure truth! That is why we should long for it in our own lives.

That is how we Christians ought to respond to the word of God. We should make the pursuit of God's word primary in our lives as if our lives depended on its consumption. This command "long for" means "to long for greatly" or "to crave." The craving is a sign of a healthy baby. Longing for the word means not being satisfied until you get the word, the whole word, and nothing but the word!

Believers need to imitate Mary of Bethany in LUKE 10:39 who sat at the feet of the Lord closely so she could hear all His teaching and miss none of it. She did not want distractions. She wanted the word! What a heart for the word she had! Jesus praised her and used her example to teach that only one thing in life was needful: The word of God! Job also declared in Job 23:12, *"I have not departed from the command of [God's] lips; I have treasured the words of His mouth more than my necessary food."*

Imagine a ward of babies where none of them desired milk. They turned their cheeks away when it was offered. "Call the doctor!" someone might worriedly exclaim. "Something is wrong with those babies!" Unfortunately, that's how many Christians and churches act. They are content with dribbles of the word amidst high-sounding, fluffy messages not teaching the Bible well. They are so filled with things of the world—with envy and hypocrisy and malice and slander and lusts and other sins—that they do not want to hear the word. Paul warned Timothy in 2 Timothy 4, *"Preach the word ... for the time will come when they will not endure sound teaching but wanting to have their ears tickled they will accumulate teachers in accordance with their own desires and will turn their ears from the truth and will turn aside to myths."* Yet we are exhorted in 2 Peter 3:18 to *"grow in the grace and knowledge of our Lord and Savior Jesus Christ."*

2 Thessalonians 1:3 also tells us, *"We ought always to give thanks to God for you, brethren, as is only fitting, because your faith is greatly enlarged, and the love of each one of you toward one another grows ever greater."* Love flows out of faith, and faith can grow by hearing the word of Christ.

In Matthew 6:30–33 Jesus spoke of small or little faith. It is a term Jesus always applied to disciples, not to unbelievers. True faith in Jesus Christ can grow and increase in a believer's life. A lesser faith allows for too much doubt, fear, insecurity, and anxiety. This weak faith leads to other sins. However, greater faith in Jesus brings peace for life and an ability to seek God's kingdom first.

Discussion & Application

1. What are some marks in your life that indicate you are longing for the word of God?

_____

_____

_____

2. How does God's word help your faith to grow?

_____

_____

_____

3. How does a growing faith help you to live the Christian life more strongly?

_____

_____

_____

Further Exploration

Mark 9:24; Romans 10:17; Colossians 3:16;
1 Thessalonians 2:13; 3:2; 5:8; 1 Timothy 4:12; 6:12;
2 Peter 1:5; Jude 20

Suggested Memory Verse

MATTHEW 4:4 _"Man shall not live on bread alone, but on every word that proceeds out of the mouth of God."_

STUDY

2

FOLLOWING & FULLNESS

LESSONS 5-8

5

REAL CHRISTIANS FOLLOW JESUS

By following Jesus as Master & Teacher, true disciples bow to His authority, learn from His example, and pattern their lives after His life.

Scriptural Teaching

MATTHEW 10:24–25 *"A disciple is not above his teacher, nor a slave above his master. It is enough for the disciple that he become like his teacher, and the slave like his master."*

This Scripture is part of the discourse on discipleship which Jesus taught to His twelve disciples earlier in His Galilean ministry. The main purpose of the discourse is to explain what true discipleship involves. In these two verses in particular, Jesus instructs the disciples what it means to follow Him. Since many people have distorted ideas about what it means to be a Christians (a follower of Christ), by turning to Jesus' teachings we clear up any confusion.

So, we may ask: What are real Christians like? If you poke them, squeeze them, shake them, what do they look and feel like? What properties do they all share? How can you tell a counterfeit from the real thing? Though Christians have different personalities, strengths, and backgrounds, all Christians hold in common certain characteristics. From this text Jesus taught three dominant characteristics all true disciples possess.

First Characteristic: Learning

Following Jesus means that the disciple desires to learn and apply Christ's teaching to his own life. *"A disciple is not above his teacher ..."* This truth was spoken to the twelve disciples, but it is meant as a general principle for any disciple, because it sets forth the basic relationship between a disciple and a teacher. A disciple is not above (not higher than, not greater than) the teacher. On the contrary, the teacher is above the disciple, and he is the greater one. That is just the way the relationship works between teachers and disciples.

In those days the teachers in Israel, the Jewish rabbis, would typically be followed by a group of students in what would be considered a portable school. Those students or pupils were the rabbi's disciples. In the common Greek language of the New Testament, that is what the word disciple, *mathetes*, meant—a learner, a pupil, a student. Disciples literally followed their teachers wherever they traveled, and they learned from their teaching in various settings. They continually sat under the rabbi's teachings and applied themselves to learn. So the student was beneath the teacher in authority and knowledge. This inferiority is inherent in the concept of being a disciple.

Consider, therefore, that to be a disciple of Jesus means to put yourself under His teaching and doctrine. It is to invite Him to teach you all about life, God, righteousness, and His kingdom. It is to absorb His doctrine willingly into the fabric of your life. No one can be a disciple of Jesus without being a student of His teachings in the New Testament.

Second Characteristic: Submission

Along with learning, a true disciple submits to what is taught. Jesus pointed this out in v. 24. He declared, "... *nor a slave above his master.*" Who was Jesus referring to as the slave? This corresponds with the disciple! Who is the master? Jesus, the teacher, is the master! Just as the disciple/teacher relationship involves instruction and learning, so the relationship of a slave to master involves submission and authority.

Slaves were bound by law to obey their masters. It was quite common in New Testament times, even in the land of Israel, to observe slaves carrying out the orders of their masters. The master had the right to give orders and expect the slave to submit to those commands. Inherent in the idea of slavery was inferiority. The masters were in control and wielded authority. The masters were greater! Again, that was just the way things were in society.

So, Jesus taught His disciples that to follow Him meant to become submissive to Him as slaves would be to their masters. In applying this to ourselves, Master Jesus should be submitted to in every area of our lives. You must not withhold an area of your life and keep it away from His authority. We accepted a relationship of submission when we came to believe in Jesus and follow Him. Submission is part of what it means to follow Jesus as Lord and Master.

Third Characteristic: Imitation

In v. 25a Jesus added, "*It is enough for the disciple that he become like his teacher, and the slave like his master.*" This expresses the goal of the disciple and the slave—to emulate the teacher and master closely. "To become like" refers to the outcome of imitation. One imitates until one becomes like another. Imitation of the master is the main purpose for being a disciple. In our case, it means we follow Christ with the intent of becoming like Him.

That is one reason Jesus let His disciples live so close to Him. He wanted them to see how He interacted with people, how He ministered to the needy, how He prayed wisely, and how He lived in holiness in all circumstances of life. Jesus put it this way in LUKE 6:40, *"A pupil is not above his teacher; but everyone, after he has been fully trained, will be like his teacher."* Full training leads to full emulation.

From the moment we place our faith in Jesus and are saved, we enter a training process, the goal of which is to become like Jesus. We are being conformed day by day into the image of Christ. Discipleship is a process of becoming more Christlike. 1 JOHN 2:6 says, *"The one who says he abides in Him ought himself to walk in the same manner as He walked."* Simply put, we should pattern ourselves after Jesus. 1 PETER 2:21 says, *"For you have been called for this purpose, since Christ also suffered for you, leaving you an example for you to follow in His steps."* There it is! Discipleship is following in Jesus' steps.

One way that is done presently is by imitating other believers who are also following Christ. Paul wrote in 1 CORINTHIANS 11:1, *"Be imitators of me, just as I also am of Christ."* Church leaders and mature believers are to take the advice given to Timothy in 1 TIMOTHY 4:12: *"Let no one look down on your youthfulness, but rather in speech, conduct, love, faith and purity, show yourself an example of those who believe."* Real Christians want to emulate Jesus and pattern themselves after those who are emulating Jesus. Christlikeness should be the goal of every Christian.

In our day, many claims to have a personal relationship with God and Christ but are not students of the teachings of Christ in Holy Scripture. As we have seen, there is no such thing as a Christian who is not a disciple of Jesus Christ. The term "disciple" is used in the Book of Acts to refer to all the Christians. "Disciple" is a synonym for "believer." In ACTS 6:2 it records, *"The twelve summoned the congregation of the disciples."* That was just another way of saying they summoned the whole church congregation. If you were in the church, you were a disciple. ACTS 11:26 informs us, *"The disciples were first called Christians in Antioch."* Christians were disciples. Disciples were Christians. Real Christians come to Jesus, not just to be saved, but to learn and to be changed by Jesus' teachings because they love and honor Him as their Master. Christians want to be like Christ.

Discussion & Application

1. In what specific ways do you truly desire to be more like Jesus?

_____

_____

_____

_____

2. When you think about being a disciple of Jesus, what is the most enjoyable part of imitating Him?

_____

_____

_____

_____

_____

3. How can you be a follower of Jesus when you cannot physically see Him right now?

_____

_____

_____

_____

_____

Key Terms/Phrases

Discipleship = the process of following Jesus and becoming like Him

Characteristics = attributes of someone which make them what they are

Christians = people who are learning from and becoming like Christ

Christ-like = the state of being like Christ in character and motives

Congregation of the disciples = another way of referring to Christians who meet together; Christians are disciples

Further Exploration

Mark 1:17; 8:34; Luke 9:59; John 1:43; 10:27; 12:26; 13:12–17; Acts 6:7; 9:26; Hebrews 13:7; 3 John 11

Suggested Memory Verse

1 JOHN 2:6 *"The one who says he abides in Him ought himself to walk in the same manner as He walked."*

FOLLOWING:
LESSON

OBEDIENCE IS THE ACTION OF FOLLOWING CHRIST

> Following Christ is measured by a growing obedience to Christ's commands and submission to God's will. Our goal should be to become more obedient to our Lord and Savior Jesus Christ

Scriptural Teaching

1 PETER 1:1–2 *"Peter, an apostle of Jesus Christ, To those who reside as aliens, scattered throughout Pontus, Galatia, Cappadocia, Asia, and Bithynia, who are chosen according to the foreknowledge of God the Father, by the sanctifying work of the Spirit, to obey Jesus Christ and be sprinkled with His blood: May grace and peace be yours in the fullest measure."*

This verse describes all believers as those *"who are chosen … [by God] … to obey Jesus Christ."* Do you ever wonder why God called you to be a Christian? What was His purpose in saving you? Was it primarily to rescue you from eternal pain and shame? Here Peter provides the answer! He saved you so you would obey Jesus

30

Christ. "That you may obey" literally is expressed by a preposition in Greek which means "unto" obeying Jesus Christ. This preposition expresses the purpose of God choosing us. A saved life is a life designed for obedience to Jesus Christ.

Obedience is what God wants from your life now that you are one of His followers. It is why God saved you. In a world where free, independent, autonomous, self-expression is highly valued and practiced, the Bible, in contrast, urges careful submission and heartfelt obedience, not to your own will, but to the will of God. God saves a soul, not to leave it to follow its own free path, but to become joyfully obedient to Jesus Christ. Indeed, the obedient person will find out that obedience to Christ is true freedom!

Coming to believe in Jesus as God's Son was the first act of obedience God required from you. 1 JOHN 3:23 points out that faith itself is obedience to a command: *"This is God's commandment that we believe in the name of His Son Jesus Christ."* Therefore, anyone who does not believe in Jesus is disobedient to God's command. JOHN 3:36 says, *"He who believes in the Son has eternal life; but he who does not obey the Son will not see life, but the wrath of God abides on him."*

Believing is an act of obedience, but it is only the first act of obedience. As we grow in our relationship with God and our love for Jesus, we will increasingly want to do the things Christ instructs us to do. JOHN 14:21 says, *"He who has my commandments and keeps them he it is who loves Me."* Furthermore, as we learned in a previous lesson, obeying Jesus accompanies calling Him Lord. LUKE 6:46–49, *"Why do you call Me, 'Lord, Lord,' and do not do what I say?"*

The Apostle Paul understood that his ministry of preaching the gospel and converting people to Christianity was meant to bring out obedience among the Gentile world. (Gentiles are all the non-Jews who were wholly disobedient to God's Law.) ROMANS 1:5 says, *"Through whom we have received grace and apostleship to bring about the obedience of faith among all the Gentiles for His name's sake."* Paul received grace and apostleship to bring about the obedience of faith among all the Gentiles (all the nations). The *"obedience of faith"* means the obedience "which springs from faith." In other words, obedience is the natural result of true faith in Jesus. We are saved by God's marvelous love and grace. Once we experience His mercy, we want to obey Him.

Even in the Great Commission, Jesus' intent for new converts after baptism was for them to be taught *"to obey all that I commanded you."* That will be the response of a heart grateful to God for being saved. That is why Paul also wrote ROMANS 15:18, *"For I will not presume to speak of anything except what Christ has accomplished through me, resulting in the obedience of the Gentiles by word and deed."* Obedience can never be divorced from faith, and faith can never be severed from obedience. Obedience is what God desires of believers.

Clearly it was never God's intent that He save us merely to have us read the Bible or to listen to it preached. We need to do what we are taught. JAMES 1:22 exhorts Christians, *"But prove yourselves doers of the word, and not merely hearers who delude themselves."* Believers are to practice what Scripture commands. Only obedience benefits us and honors God. Listening to God's word without obedience is self-deceptive. People can delude themselves into thinking that they are growing closer to God simply because they hear a great deal of Bible teaching. Yet God's word has an inherent authority that must be acknowledged. Just as it is dishonoring to stand in the presence of a monarch, listen to his declarations, and then go home and disregard his commands, so it is with King Jesus. If His words are merely listened to and ignored, how is He truly honored?

Therefore, obedience can never be pushed off to a more advanced stage of the Christian faith. Obedience begins immediately at salvation, and it continues growing stronger as each believer walks with God throughout life.

The next act of obedience after salvation is baptism. Jesus commanded us to be baptized in water immediately after we believe. This gives a public affirmation of our faith. All the new converts in ACTS 2 were baptized in water in the name of Jesus. Jesus commanded all who believed to be baptized *"in the name of the Father, the Son, and the Holy Spirit"* (MATTHEW 28:19). The Ethiopian Eunuch knew he was to be baptized immediately upon believing in Jesus in ACTS 8:36.

Peter also taught the importance of obedience for all God's children. In 1 PETER 1:14 we read, *"As obedient children, do not be conformed to the former lusts which were yours in your ignorance, but like the Holy One who called you be holy also yourselves in all your behavior. For it is written, 'You shall be holy for I the Lord your God am Holy.'"* Literally the first phrase in that verse is "children of obedience," which is a stronger way of describing our relationship to obedience. Obedience is so much a part of God's children, it characterizes them. Conversely, disobedience characterizes the unbeliever. EPHESIANS 2:2 calls unbelievers *"sons of disobedience"* because a continuous flow of disobedient actions, words, and attitudes characterizes their lives. Obviously, nobody wants to have disobedient children, and that includes God. PROVERBS 10:1 says, *"A wise son makes a father glad, but a foolish son is a grief to his mother."* God also wants wise, obedient children who reflect His character, trust Him, and rejoice in doing His will.

This is a good place to do a self-check: Are you an obedient child of God? God commands us to forgive each other (EPHESIANS 4:32). Are you holding a grudge against someone right now? It is God's command that we tell others about Jesus (ACTS 1:8). Do you open your mouth and speak the gospel to others? It is God's will that we join a church and fellowship with others (ACTS 2:42F). Are you dedicated to a church in which to learn and serve your brothers and sisters in Christ? It is God's will that you be baptized to show others that you now believe

(ACTS 2:38; MATT 28:18–20; ACTS 8:36–39). Have you been baptized since you believed? It is the Bible's teaching that you do not lie, steal, get drunk, swear at others, or be lazy at work (EPHESIANS 4:25–32; 5:18). Are you obeying God's teachings in these areas too?

These are just some of the instructions given to NT believers. As you learn more of the word, you will gain more wisdom putting into practice what you learn and be blessed by God as you obey.

Discussion & Application

1. Have you seen a change in your desire to obey the Bible since you believed in Jesus? In what ways?

_____

_____

_____

_____

2. In what important areas of your life do you need to learn obedience to the commands of Jesus?

_____

_____

_____

_____

3. Why does a true Christian want to obey Jesus Christ? Why does a Christian feel bad when he/she disobeys Christ?

_____

_____

_____

_____

Key Terms/Phrases

The Obedience of Faith = obedient actions toward Jesus stemming from faith

An Obedient Child = a child who listens to his father and does what he says; related to God as our Father

Baptism = immersion in water as the first sign of obedience to our new master Jesus

Great Commission = Jesus' lofty commission to the church to make disciples of all the nations

Chosen to Obey = God selected us to be saved with the greater purpose of our obedience to Him

Further Exploration

John 13:17; Acts 5:29; 6:7; Romans 6:12–16; 2 Corinthians 10:5; Philippians 2:8, 12; Hebrews 5:9; 11:8; James 4:7; 1 Peter 1:22

Suggested Memory Verse

JOHN 14:21 *"He who has My commandments and keeps them is the one who loves Me ..."*

FULLNESS:
LESSON

7

FILLED WITH THE HOLY SPIRIT OF GOD

Since Christ gave His followers the Holy Spirit to energize, empower, and lead the Christian life into more obedience, Christians should fully avail themselves of His powerful influence so they can walk in His ways.

Scriptural Teaching

EPHESIANS 5:18 *"And do not get drunk with wine, for that is dissipation, but be filled with the Spirit."*

The New Testament makes it clear that Christians are to be filled with the Holy Spirit. What is the filling of the Holy Spirit, and how can we be filled with the Spirit?

To understand the filling of the Spirit we must consider the contrast Paul is making in the verse. Note the word *"but"* in the middle. *"Do not get drunk with wine, BUT be filled with the Spirit."* The contrast is between drunkenness due to an abundance of wine that works as a depressant, minimizing our thinking and hindering the physical body, and the Holy Spirit who acts as a stimulant, flooding believers with energy and divine wisdom. So this

36

exhortation is for our good. God wants us filled with His Spirit, not wine, because the results are far better. God gives believers this command because He wants to rescue us from lesser sensual pleasures and graciously bestow on us a better state of existence. The Spirit brings to us, as Jesus promised, rivers of living water bubbling up within our souls (JOHN 7:37–39). Though the word "holy" is absent from v. 18, elsewhere in EPHESIANS (see 2:22; 3:5; 6:18) this exact phrase, literally "in spirit," refers to the Holy Spirit. So we should truly desire the filling of the Holy Spirit of God in our innermost beings!

We also need to understand the verb *"be filled."* It is more exactly (and awkwardly) translated "be being filled" because it is a present command indicating a state to enter, not a one-time event to experience. The word *"filled"* is from the Greek verb *pleroo*. It describes a normal fullness of the Holy Spirit which is vitally related to our character and spiritual maturity. This metaphor "filled" or "full" does not describe a sudden welling up or a pouring in of the Spirit from the outside. The Holy Spirit already indwells believers, so they do not need the Holy Spirit to be poured into them. EPHESIANS 1:13 teaches we were all *"sealed in Christ with the Holy Spirit of promise."* So there is no such thing as a believer without the Spirit or with more of the Spirit than another. Rather, this filling describes a permeating influence of the Holy Spirit whereby your whole life, like a sponge, can be saturated with the power, joy, godliness, influence, and fruit of the Holy Spirit. One who is full of the Holy Spirit is one who reflects the character and priorities of the Holy Spirit. In this state of fullness, the person is also more like Jesus Christ. In the context of EPHESIANS 5:15–17, the fullness of the Spirit also means to walk through life under the Spirit's leadership so that you may be wise and make the most of every opportunity for Christ to shine as lights in a dark world.

ACTS 13:52 describes the Christian disciples as *"continually filled with joy and with the Holy Spirit."* In ACTS 11:24 Barnabas is described as a good man and *"full of the Holy Spirit."* So being full of the Spirit does not mean being filled like filling the gas tank or filling a cup of coffee to the brim. It means to be permeated by, to be influenced by, to be moved along by the Holy Spirit of God so you live like Jesus. That means this kind of filling of the Spirit is gradual. Unlike other times where the Spirit filled certain people rapidly to prophecy or do miracles, this kind comes in degrees and results in gradual Christlikeness.

Notice also that this command is a passive verb not an active one. It may seem strange to receive a passive command, yet the idea is instructive. Paul is not commanding us to fill ourselves with the Spirit, but to let ourselves be continuously filled by God. God, the Holy Spirit, does the active saturating. We let ourselves be filled by Him by opening up our lives to Him more and more. Interestingly, both verbs in v. 18 are in the passive: "Do not give yourself to drunkenness but give yourself to being filled by the Spirit." Rather than sitting at a bar and letting ourselves get drunk, we should let the Spirit permeate our thinking, our lives, our entire beings. Though the verb is passive, notice that Paul puts the responsibility to be filled on us not on God. God stands ready to fill us and to bring us to the fullness; we must give way to Him. So, this is really a command about yielding. Yield the right-of-way to God's Spirit. Let Him take over and move your life along the way He wants. Do not fill your life with other things that tantalize and entertain but do not make you godly. The effect of drunkenness is harmful. The Spirit's fullness is blessed!

This exhortation is similar to GALATIANS 5:16 where we are also commanded, *"Walk by the Spirit and you will not carry out the desire of the flesh."* To walk by the Spirit means to get in step with what the Holy Spirit is doing inside you. When you do that, the sins from your selfish flesh will be minimized. Too often we think that the spiritual life will come quickly and easily. The error of the less mature Christian is that he wants to be zapped and instantly sanctified. He wants to have the Spirit energize him while requiring no ongoing obedience, little discipline, and no daily dying to self. Yet walking by the Spirit speaks of constancy. A walk takes time. There are no short cuts. Being full of God's Spirit requires a constant dedication to your spiritual steps. All week long you have influences working to draw you away from your spiritual walk with Christ. The more you pay close attention to your walk, the more you will find that He is the one who wells up within you to spread blessing to your entire being. Your life will be like a sailboat with the sail uplifted. The Spirit will fill your sails and push you along your journey! God will fill your submission to Him with His divine, holy wind. However, if you pull the sail back down due to self-will and weak faith, the wind will not avail you.

So "be being filled" is a command urging constancy in the Spirit of God, not just a one-time dose of the Spirit. Drink a full dose of the Spirit all day long. In a parallel passage Paul urges in COLOSSIANS 3:16, *"Let the word of Christ richly dwell within you, with all wisdom teaching and admonishing one another with psalms and hymns and spiritual songs, singing with thankfulness in your hearts to God."* The word of the Spirit richly dwelling in you also brings the permeating influence of the Spirit of God.

Discussion & Application

1. How are you aware of your relationship to the Holy Spirit throughout the day and week as you walk with Christ?

_____

_____

_____

2. How are being full of the Spirit and walking in the Spirit similar?

_____

_____

_____

3. Specifically, would spiritual disciplines like prayer and Scripture-reading aid you in being full of God's Spirit? Why?

_____

_____

_____

Key Terms/Phrases

Filling of the Holy Spirit = the state of being controlled by the Spirit of God rather than worldly influences

The Holy Spirit = the Spirit of God who is a person and God; He flows from God and is God Himself

The Christian Walk = daily living as a Christian; step by step progress in living the Christian faith

Dying to Self = learning to say "No" to your own desires and will so you can do the will of God

Fruit of the Holy Spirit = the good character the Holy Spirit produces in the life of a believer

Further Exploration

Romans 5:5; 8:14; 14:17; 15:13; 1 Corinthians 3:16;
2 Corinthians 3:17; Ephesians 4:30; 6:18; Philippians 1:19;
1 Thessalonians 1:5–6

Suggested Memory Verse

COLOSSIANS 3:16 "*Let the word of Christ richly dwell within you, with all wisdom teaching and admonishing one another with psalms and hymns and spiritual songs, singing with thankfulness in your hearts to God.*"

THE HOLY SPIRIT GIVES POWER TO BATTLE THE FLESH

The indwelling Holy Spirit transforms believers
to live like Christ. He effectively leads Christians
to put off deeds of the sinful flesh

Scriptural Teaching

ROMANS 8:12 *"So then, brethren, we are under obligation, not to the flesh, to live according to the flesh."*

The verses before this one in ROMANS 8 teach that the Holy Spirit lives within each believer, and He produces in us a "mind-set" to do God's will. This way we are able to resist the lures of our sinful flesh. Verse 12 then points to the logical consequences of His indwelling. Since the Spirit of God lives in us, we are under obligation to the Spirit not to the sinful flesh. The term *"obligation"* means literally a debtor; one owing goods or money. Not to be a debtor to the flesh means that we do not have to obey the flesh and follow its dictates. We owe the sinful flesh nothing. We are under new obligation as to how to live our lives since we have been given God's Spirit. 1 CORINTHIANS 6:19 reminds us, *"Or do you not know that your body is a temple of the Holy Spirit who is in you, whom you have from God, and that you are not your own? Therefore, glorify God in your body."* EPHESIANS 1:13 tells us that Christians *"were sealed in Him with the Holy Spirit of promise."* Erdman in his commentary summarizes it this way: "Every day has its battles for a follower of Christ, every hour its struggle; but by trustful surrender to the Holy Spirit, constant victory can be enjoyed."

ROMANS 8:13 *"...for if you are living according to the flesh, you must die; but if by the Spirit you are putting to death the deeds of the body, you will live."* Those who live carnally (in a continuously sinful manner) will not gain eternal life but eternal death. That tells us that true Christians do not continuously live like they did before coming to faith in Christ. So sanctification (cleaning us up and setting us apart for God) by the Spirit is not a luxury but a necessity that always accompanies salvation. Those who are not going through the process of being sanctified by God's Spirit are not saved, and they do not have the Holy Spirit inside them. The conjunction "but" in the verse contrasts living by the Spirit with living by the flesh. The flesh and Spirit are opposed to one another. This verse clearly describes the battle against the sinful flesh that the believer in Jesus experiences. The believer is one who is putting to death the deeds of the flesh. The deeds refer to practices or actions or habits of the sinful flesh. Putting to death the deeds refers to killing them off one by one. It is a hard, continuous, battle, but it is a progressive and winning battle.

We call this the mortification of the sinful flesh. Mortification does not mean harming the physical body but putting off sinful practices in our lives. It is only when we live by the Spirit that we are able to put to death the deeds of the body. The sinful flesh has already been crucified and is dead, in the sense that its power is gone. It is no longer in control of our lives. However, the flesh still kicks and screams trying to act like it retains power. It has no real power, because the believer has the power now to put to death the deeds of the flesh by the indwelling and sanctifying ministry of the Holy Spirit. So, in one sense the believer has already died to sin, and the old self is crucified. ROMANS 6:2 says, *"How shall we who died to sin still live in it?"* In another sense, the Christian must believe that the flesh is powerless over the work of God's Spirit, and, in that confidence, put to death its practices in life. Dr. John MacArthur in his book *The Vanishing Conscience* writes:

> Mortification involves the cultivation of new habits of godliness, combined with the elimination of old sinful habits from our behavior. It is a constant warfare that takes place within the believer ... The instrument of mortification is the Holy Spirit, and His power is the energy that works in us to carry out the process. All the means of mortification are simple commands of Scripture that we are to obey.

ROMANS 8:14 *"For all who are being led by the Spirit of God, these are sons of God."* Being led by the Spirit expresses a Greek verb in the present tense. That means it is something the Spirit is doing presently for every believer. The term "led" means "to bring" or, in some cases, "to draw or to compel" someone to come along. Some people think of the leading of the Spirit as mystical communication or even whispers the Spirit gives to believers to help them know how to make important decisions in life. However, you can tell from the context that this "leading" does not refer to the Spirit of God giving people guidance for individual life decisions. The leading of the Spirit is not a subjective way to determine who to marry, where to go to church, or which job to accept. The context in ROMANS 8 is not about deciphering God's individual will for one's life. Instead, the leading of the Holy Spirit is more profound, powerful, and basic. The Spirit is bringing us along in the direction He wants us to go. Do you remember what that direction is? Christlikeness! The leading empowers the mortification of the deeds of the sinful flesh and our ability to put on Christ-like attitudes, character, and habits. The leading of the Spirit indicates that the primary power and strength in the Christian life is not you or your will power, but God's Spirit.

The leading of the Spirit also brings assurance to every believer. All those led by the Spirit are also those who are sons of God. This way the leading of the Spirit brings assurance that we are children of God. GALATIANS 4:6 says, *"Because you are sons, God has sent forth the Spirit of His Son into our hearts, crying, 'Abba! Father!'"* Leading, empowerment, and assurance of the Spirit work together. The further the Spirit of God leads you, the more He changes you to be like Christ. That transformation in turn brings Christians assurance that they are truly one of God's children transformed by the power of the resident Holy Spirit.

Discussion & Application

1. Why does a believer need the power of the Spirit to lay off sinful practices?

_____

_____

_____

_____

_____

2. Describe the internal battle going on between God's Spirit and the flesh? Who is winning and why?

_____

_____

_____

_____

_____

3. How does the leading of the Spirit bring assurance of our salvation?

_____

_____

_____

_____

Key Terms/Phrases

Led by the Spirit = the Holy Spirit's leadership to conform us to the image of Jesus Christ

Mortification of the Flesh = putting to death the sinful deeds we do in our bodies

The Flesh = not simply the human body, but the evil residing in our human flesh

Glorify God in Your Body = bringing honor to God by the way you live in your body

Died to Sin = the definitive break from the power of sin in our lives when Jesus became our Master

Further Exploration

Romans 6:8–14; 2 Corinthians 3:17–18; Galatians 6:8;
Ephesians 1:13–14; 3:16–17; 1 Thessalonians 4:3

Suggested Memory Verse

1 CORINTHIANS 6:19–20 "Or do you not know that your body is a
temple of the Holy Spirit who is in you, whom you have from God,
and that you are not your own? For you have been bought with a
price: therefore glorify God in your body."

Notes

John Mac Arthur, The Vanishing Conscience (Dallas, Word Publishing)
p.156, 157

STUDY

3

FELLOWSHIP & FEARING
LESSONS 9-12

THE JOY AND BLESSINGS OF CHRISTIAN FELLOWSHIP

Christians were designed to be in constant fellowship
with other believers, serving Christ together,
and strengthened by quality Christian relationships
within the local church.

Scriptural Teaching

ACTS 2:42–47 *"They were continually devoting themselves to
the apostles' teaching and to fellowship, to the breaking of
bread and to prayer. Everyone kept feeling a sense of awe;
and many wonders and signs were taking place through the
apostles. And all those who had believed were together and
had all things in common; and they began selling their property and possessions and were sharing them with all, as anyone might have need. Day by day continuing with one mind
in the temple, and breaking bread from house to house, they
were taking their meals together with gladness and sincerity
of heart, praising God and having favor with all the people.
And the Lord was adding to their number day by day those
who were being saved."*

Our American culture has shaped us in more ways than we realize. Sometimes culture influences us negatively in imperceptible ways.

American culture, for example, values privacy. That is not a bad thing in itself. We enjoy our space and our right to live life shielded from the watchful eye of others. This desire for privacy, however, can tend toward isolationism rather than communal living. Isolationism, in turn, tends to coldness between neighbors as we each become more preoccupied with our own comfort, pleasure, and quiet rather than meaningful interaction with others. Selfishness, in turn, produces loneliness, since quality relationships are sacrificed for peace and quiet.

Furthermore, culturally speaking, Americans are used to having multiple choices. We expect variety in many areas of life, from the brand of cereal we prefer, to the banking options we expect, to even the type of study Bible that best fits our spiritual needs. We expect life to be tailored to our needs. The unintended fallout from that is that we typically do not do well when we are asked to sacrifice.

Americans also tend to be materialistic and self-sufficient. In many of our homes we were taught hard work, rugged individualism, the American Dream, and self-reliance, but those things can lead to a preoccupation with physical blessings rather than spiritual pursuits. What we own can become more important to us than exhibiting godly character.

The combination of these cultural influences tends to reduce our commitment to one another and to our church. As the church's sense of love and commitment to one another wanes, Christians hold back their loving commitment to other believers. This in turn leads them to feel free to bounce from church to church or Bible study to Bible study as it suits their schedules and needs. Some believers do not see the importance of commitment and just stay home or listen online.

However, God intended the church to be different from the cold, materialistic, and withdrawn society which surrounds us! He designed the church to be a model of right relationships and priorities amidst a larger society, which has lost its way.

In ACTS 2:42–47 we read that the first local church, founded in Jerusalem, was a distinct society from the surrounding unbelievers. They were different from the cold, ritualistic Judaism prevalent in that day. This early church was a godly and dynamic example of loving, interactive relationships centered on Christ, His word, and His work. Verse 42 states, "[The new Christians] *were continually devoting themselves to the apostles' doctrine and to the fellowship ...*" Their commitment to learn the word of God instilled in them a love for one another and a desire to be a true fellowship of believers. That is a healthy model of fellowship for us to emulate.

The word in the New Testament translated "fellowship" is *koin nia*. It means partnership or sharing. Fellowship involves a mutual action and common interest. Christian fellowship is referenced in 1 JOHN 1:3 which says that the apostles proclaimed eternal life to the rest of the world, "*so that you also may have fellowship with us; and indeed our fellowship is with the Father, and with His Son Jesus Christ.*" Eternal life, then, is something to be shared among believers. Christian fellowship is a sharing in the eternal life we have together with God and Christ.

That means fellowship is more encompassing than simply time around doughnuts and coffee. Fellowship runs broader and deeper. It is the sharing of the whole Christian life and every aspect of it with other followers of Christ. We believers share a life of a common Lord, Spirit, baptism, faith, confession, hope, worship, and service. Visibly this fellowship is pictured as we regularly gather around the Lord's Table (a time we call communion), but we also share life around the word, prayer, evangelism, ministry, and spiritual songs. When believers are together, we have so much to enjoy and share because of our shared eternal life.

Because of this shared life, when we gather together, whether it is formal church on Sundays or some other time, we should center our attention and conversation on the kingdom of Christ and not waste significant time discussing politics, sports, new apps, or the latest movies. We have a deeper and better connection—the greatness of God's promises, the excellencies of Jesus Christ, and the fellowship of the Holy Spirit!

Luke, the author of Acts, goes on to describe the fellowship these early believers enjoyed with each other. ACTS 2:44–46 says, *"And all those who had believed were together, and had all things in common; and they began selling their property and possessions, and were sharing them with all, as anyone might have need. And day by day continuing with one mind in the temple, and breaking bread from house to house, they were taking their meals together with gladness and sincerity of heart."* At this early stage of church history, the disciples were together in Jerusalem and met daily in the temple. They also had fellowship from house to house sharing meals together and taking the Lord's Supper to remember and proclaim Christ's death. They were conversing with one another, enjoying each other, and witnessing together. Wherever you saw one disciple you saw a bunch. They were birds of a feather, and they flocked for Christ together. Each believer was associated with the others.

They not only were together, but v. 44 states that they had *"all things in common."* They mutually cared for one another in tangible ways. This was not forced socialism or required giving but voluntary sharing. Physical needs were met within the community as a tangible expression of their common life.

We Christians today also have a common life to live for a common Lord. We should not think of ourselves as merely attending church or going to church on Sundays. Rather we should always remember that WE ARE the church, all day and every day! We never stop being the church. The church is our identity, for the church is "in Christ." The church is about the relationship we have with Christ and one another. That is why HEBREWS 10:24–25 exhorts, *"Let us consider how to stimulate one another to love and good deeds, not forsaking our own assembling together, as is the habit of some, but encouraging one another; and all the more, as you see the day drawing near."* ROMANS 12:10 urges, *"Be devoted to one another in brotherly love; giving preference to one another in honor."* ROMANS 12:16 implores, *"Be of the same mind toward one another; do not be haughty in mind, but associate with the lowly ..."* Those exhortations, and many like them in the New Testament, compel us to be a people dedicated to Christian fellowship.

The description of this early community continues in v. 46, *"taking their meals together with gladness and sincerity of heart."* What an atmosphere this fellowship produced! Their hearts were unhindered before the Lord. They served and worshiped sincerely. This church had character! It was a joyful church, not a drab or complacent church. An obedient, loving, and Spirit-filled church will always be joyful.

Let us remember that God has not only saved us individually but connected us corporately. The church is the body of Jesus Christ upon earth. We each have our connection to the body and our part in the body to perform. Let us commit ourselves to function like it and experience the joy that the Lord intended.

Discussion & Application

1. What is Christian fellowship, and how is its meaning sometimes minimized or reduced?

_____

_____

_____

_____

2. Why is the Christian life lived better when we practice Christian fellowship?

_____

_____

_____

_____

3. In what specific ways can you increase your Christian fellowship time?

_____

_____

_____

_____

Key Terms/Phrases

Fellowship = the common life we share in Christ in all its dimensions and activities

The Lord's Supper = an ordinance Christians are to practice to remember Christ and share in fellowship

Eternal Life = life from God given through Christ and lasting forever

Church = the collection of all believers who regularly gather together for the word and fellowship

Further Exploration

Acts 14:22; 1 Corinthians 1:9; 2 Corinthians 6:14; 13:14; Ephesians 4:11–16; Philippians 2:1–4; 1 Thessalonians 5:11; Hebrews 3:13

Suggested Memory Verse

HEBREWS 10:24–25 "*Let us consider how to stimulate one another to love and good deeds, not forsaking our own assembling together, as is the habit of some, but encouraging one another; and all the more, as you see the day drawing near.*"

BELIEVERS ARE MEMBERS OF CHRIST'S BODY, THE CHURCH

As members of Christ's body, we are designed to live the Christian life cooperatively and dependently not individualistically or independently.

Scriptural Teaching

1 CORINTHIANS 12:12 "For even as the body is one and yet has many members, and all the members of the body, though they are many, are one body, so also is Christ."

FIRST CORINTHIANS 12 is the preeminent passage in the New Testament about the interconnectivity of the body of Christ particularly through the use of diverse spiritual gifts. The Holy Spirit bestows upon each believer a different spiritual ability, then places that believer in the spiritual body of Christ to use that gift for the benefit of the whole body. Paul summarizes in 1 CORINTHIANS 12:12f the three main truths he aims to instill in believers from this passage. These truths are the bedrock that undergirds the need for Christian fellowship.

First, Paul declares there is only one body of Christ even though there are many members in the body. The amazing diversity of the body is seen in Paul's use of diverse couplets—the foot & the hand, the ear & the eye, the head & the feet, the weak members & the strong members. This passage illustrates the truth expressed in EPHESIANS 4:15–16 "... *speaking the truth in love we are to grow up into all aspects into Him, who is the head, even Christ, from whom the whole body, being fitted and held together by that which every joint supplies, according to the proper working of each individual part, causes the growth of the body for the building up of itself in love."*

In 1 CORINTHIANS 12:14–19 Paul teaches that the one body has many different members. Each of these members performs a needed function in the body. The foot and the hand are different, but both are equally part of the body. Every different function of the body is there because God placed it there and it is needed. That means no inferiority complexes are allowed in the church. You are needed in the body because you are a member.

Paul's question in v. 19 proves his point, *"If they were all one member, where would the body be?"* There would be no wisdom in gifting every Christian the same way! The one body needs many different members which are designed to do different functions but to work together. We are to remain unified in our work and service because we are one body.

In vv. 15–19 Paul tells us to recognize the value of our own position and gift within the body. God put you in the body. The other parts of God's church need you too, for without you the body is incomplete. You have no right, therefore, to remove yourself from where God connected you. So do not minimize God's gift given to you, and do not be envious of the gifts and spiritual abilities given to others around you. God's wisdom encourages you to just take what He has given you and use it to build up the body.

That is also why we are to have the same care for one another (1 CORINTHIANS 12:25–26). The Scripture tells us to *"rejoice with those who rejoice, and weep with those who weep"* (ROMANS 12:15); *"Pray for one another"* (JAMES 5:16); *"Forgive one another"* (EPHESIANS 4:32); *"Bear one another's burdens"* (GALATIANS 6:1). In other words, your concern should be our concern. Our trial should be your trial. Your burden should be our burden. Our pain should be your pain and your joy our joy. We should share triumphs and milestones together. The body is mutually dependent. Everyone is needed in the body!

Unfortunately, most believers seem satisfied with a lesser involvement in the body of Christ than the level Christ designed for his church. In fact, some people choose not to attend church at all, because they know if they did they would have to get more involved. Someone once left our church saying, "This church requires too much from people." However, they were hardly involved. Not to be involved in a local church is not only an act of disobedience to the Lord but reveals a complete misunderstanding about one's connection to the body of Christ. Another person once told me, "I do not need to go to church because I follow God on my own." That person was acting as if she was not a part of the body, and that is not true.

The second truth is that all the members make up the one body. In v. 20 of 1 CORINTHIANS 12 Paul states the same truth in reverse. Notice how v. 14 and v. 20 are like reverse images in a mirror. Verse 14 says the body is not one but many. Verse 20 reverses it and teaches that many members are one body. So, vv. 20–26 illustrate this reverse truth! The members have need of each other. They must work interdependently not independently. The more-seen and honored members are not more important than the less-seen and less prominent members. No division in the body can be tolerated, for division hurts the whole body. So, if one member suffers, all the members must care for it because it hurts them, too.

This is true in the human body. Have you ever had a pain in a shoulder or wrist or even in the neck? Or have you ever suffered with a bad tooth or a pain in the pinky? Even the smallest hurt can prevent the rest of the body from functioning well. This is also true with the body of Christ.

Third, the body referred to is none other than the body of Jesus Christ. Verse 27 is the focal point and the climax of this whole section in 1 CORINTHIANS 12. Here Paul takes the simple truths about the human body and drives home the relevance of this teaching to the Corinthian church and to us. *"Now you are Christ's body, and individually are members of it."* You Corinthians, and you and I today—we are Christ's own body.

These words show forth the magnificent truth that we are the living, dynamic body of Christ on earth. This is our real identity.

If you forget who you are, if you start to see yourself the way the unbelieving world around you sees you, no different from anybody else, just an American living the individual dream, then you will not live for God in the context of the church. You must never forget who you are, because what you do stems from who you are.

We are constantly exhorted in Scripture to excel in our service toward our Master, not just because He deserves it, but because of who we are—His body. We are here to glorify our head, and we are joined to each other. So life and service in church is necessary if we are going to love God with all of our heart, soul, mind, and strength.

Discussion & Application

1. Why is each Christian important to the functioning of the body of Christ?

_____

_____

_____

2. What are some excuses people make for not being more involved in the church?

_____

_____

_____

3. In what way can you serve in the body more?

_____

_____

_____

Key Terms/Phrases

The Body of Christ = the church as the expression of Christ in this world working together

Members of the Body = the individuals who make up the church, each different from the other

Spiritual Gift = spiritual ability given to each believer to help the rest of the body of Christ

Further Exploration

Romans 12:3–8,10,16; 13:8; 14:19; 15:5,7,14;
Galatians 5:13, 26; Ephesians 4:2,25,32; 5:19;
Philippians 2:3; Colossians 3:13

Suggested Memory Verse

EPHESIANS 4:15–16 "_speaking the truth in love we are to grow up into all aspects into Him, who is the head, even Christ, from whom the whole body, being fitted and held together by that which every joint supplies, according to the proper working of each individual part, causes the growth of the body for the building up of itself in love._"

WORSHIPPING GOD IN PERSONAL DEVOTIONS

Our reverent awe of God should inspire us
to spend time alone with Him every day, praising Him,
and cherishing our privileged relationship in
Christ with the Almighty.

Scriptural Teaching

PSALM 146:1–2 *"Praise the Lord! Praise the Lord, O my soul! I will praise the Lord while I live; I will sing praises to my God while I have my being."*

Since our relationship with God is crucial, the Bible encourages us to learn to praise God and spend time alone with Him in sincere worship. Some people call this personal worship time "Devotions" or a "Quiet Time." Whatever it is called, the main point is that we need to grow in our relationship with God, particularly learning to praise and thank Him for all He is and does.

The psalter reveals how godly people expressed their worship to God in prayer and song. PSALM 146:1–2 exclaims, *"Praise the LORD! Praise the LORD, O my soul! I will praise the LORD*

while I live; I will sing praises to my God while I have my being."
In the beginning of this psalm the reader senses rising emotions
as each new line intensifies the previous one. This crescendo
reflects the psalmist's growing intensity in personal worship.

In the first line, *"Praise the* LORD*!"* we hear the basic commitment of the psalmist to praise God. In Hebrew this phrase
is just one word, "Hallelujah," which is a compound word from
hallel, "to praise"; and *jah,* a shortened form of Jehovah or
Yahweh. Thus, it means "Praise Yahweh."

Hallelujah is a common word used in multiple situations in
worship of God. Believers would praise God for who He is, as
in PSALM 106:1, *"Praise the* LORD*! Oh give thanks to the* LORD,
for He is good." Believers should also praise Him for what He
does, which is merely an extension of who He is, as in PSALM
113:9, *"He makes the barren woman abide in the house as a joyful mother of children. Praise the* LORD*!"* Also, in this psalm you
can read the praise lifted up for God's beneficial actions toward
Israel. Praise, therefore, is akin to thanksgiving. The direction of
the praise and thankfulness, of course, is the Lord.

"The LORD" is the Hebrew covenant name for God—
Yahweh. God is in covenant relation with the nation of Israel.
The name comes from God's awesome declaration of self-existence to Moses on Mt. Sinai, *"I am who I am."* He described
Himself as the uncaused Being who has always existed. He is the
fountainhead of all life and existence. This is the God to whom
the Israelites bound themselves in covenant. So, in this psalm
the psalmist particularly reflects on what God means to Israel.

We also should learn to personalize our devotion time to
reflect what God means to us. Our praise should arise out of
awe for God. We should set aside undistracted time every day
to be alone with God, reflect on His power and goodness, and
then praise Him.

The second line grows more intense. *"Praise the* LORD,
O my soul!" He intensifies the praise by localizing it to his

own soul. Dr. Steve Lawson calls this statement, "an exuberant, boisterous shout to God." It is also "a sermon to yourself." This is someone calling forth his own duty toward God. Often others remind us to give thanks to God. However, here the psalmist preaches to himself, "Soul, give forth a Hallelujah!" Do you sense the emotion and passion in that statement? It is true worship from the heart! If you capture the commitment being voiced here, you can tell it is not stale, external worship. We should not have personal devotions simply as a bare, dutiful act. The daily worship of God must originate deep within your soul. Jesus taught in JOHN 4:24 we must worship God in spirit as well as truth. The Law commands us to love the Lord our God with all our heart and soul and mind. True worship comes from the heart.

The third line climbs even higher. *"I will praise the* LORD *while I live."* Here the commitment to praise takes another step up. We learn the commitment to praise extends through the duration of his life. Worshipping God is not meant to be a daily task to be checked off, but a lifetime practice and a joyful pursuit! My lifetime ambition should be to worship God. Personal worship is not about drumming up a worship mood that comes and goes. It is not merely to be a temporary excitement generated by wonderful worship music. Worship is a determination to endure throughout life, *"while I live"*—that is, to the end of my life. As long as I have life, when you see me, you will see me praising the Lord! When you get older, you should still be praising the Lord. At this point in the psalm there is no mention of the practice of others in personal worship. This is personal resolve to worship the Lord regardless of what others do. Do you have that commitment?

The fourth line brings the commitment to worship to its apex, *"I will sing praises to my God while I have my being."* My whole being will worship my God. That is what truly honors God, and that is a healthy approach to life. That is a person who knows what he is about. My being—my existence—is to worship His being, His greater existence. I, the lesser, worship Him, the greater.

My praise will also encompass music because music takes me to the heights of worship. The praise I render will be so delightful it will be put to poetry and then to song. The remaining psalms, particularly 149 and 150, bring out the cymbals, string instruments, pipes, and all the instruments joining in the chorus to give praise to the Lord. It is good to use music in your personal devotions, just like in PSALM 104:33, "*I will sing to the LORD as long as I live; I will sing praise to my God while I have my being.*" There is also no grumbling in this psalm. There are no accusations against God that He has not provided. There is unmixed devotion, focus, and worship.

Steve Lawson again comments:

> One of the most accurate measures of where any believer is spiritually is the intensity of his praise to God. A growing Christian is one who is growing in the fervency of his praise of God. Wherever there is advancement in the grace of the Lord Jesus Christ, there will be an ever-increasing sacrifice of praise ascending from his heart to the Lord ... When Jesus Christ is genuinely loved, there will be a growing surge of adoring praise. A soul enraptured with God will be evidenced by a mouth exalting him.[1]

So, let us determine to worship God in the awe of adoring worship. Let us commit to the daily joy of praising God for who He is and all He has done for us in Christ!

Discussion & Application

1. How much do you practice praising the Lord in your daily devotions?

_____

_____

_____

_____

2. How does fearing God inspire your worship of Him? What is a healthy fear of God?

_____

_____

_____

_____

3. Describe your commitment to daily devotions alone with God? What hinders you from that commitment?

_____

_____

_____

_____

Key Terms/Phrases

Worship = ascribing to God greatness and goodness; devoting oneself to God in adoration

Devotions = daily time alone with God building a stronger relationship in His word and with praise and thanksgiving

Thanksgiving = rendering to God thanks for all He is and for all He does

Psalms = the worship portion of Scripture filled with songs to teach us to praise God and give Him thanks

Further Exploration

Psalm 42:11; 103:2; 104:1; Luke 6:12; Ephesians 6:18;
Philippians 1:4; Colossians 3:16; 4:2; Hebrews 13:15;
1 Peter 3:12

Suggested Memory Verse

PSALM 146:1–2 *"Praise the LORD! Praise the LORD, O my soul! I will praise the LORD while I live; I will sing praises to my God while I have my being."*

Notes

Steven J. Lawson, *Holman Old Testament Commentary: Psalms 67–150*, vol. 12, ed. Max Anders, (Holman Reference, Nashville, TN, 2006), 361.

12

THE IMPORTANCE OF WORSHIPPING WITH OTHER BELIEVERS

Our God is honored among the praises of God's people; this honor is heightened as we worship the Lord together as a body of believers.

Scriptural Teaching

PSALM 100:2 *Serve the LORD with gladness; Come before Him with joyful singing.*

We live in a man-focused society that does not encourage true worship of God. We are bombarded with self-promoting advertisements, with man-centered philosophies, and with human-based psychologies that start and end with human insights and human fulfillment. Even in the realm of religion people twist worship to make it more about experiencing wonderful feelings and excitement than about focusing on God's majestic glory.

Despite human foolishness, we remain created beings who are only fulfilling our created purpose when we worship God! We must adore the greatness of our Creator before we can rightly know ourselves. The casualness that modern churches display in their approach to God in worship is an admission they know not the God they worship. Believers who truly immerse themselves in the greatness of God reveal their insight and find joy and fulfillment by lowering themselves before Almighty God. With this in mind, we need to be a community of believers who are truly God-centered in worship.

PSALM 100 is a call to corporate worship. Verse 1 is a summons of praise to *"all the earth,"* which fits well with the universal kingship of Yahweh described in the previous PSALMS 95–99. Like the previous psalms, this psalm is associated with the enthronement of the Lord in the temple in Israel. It serves as a doxology on the theme of Yahweh as King.

Seven commands are issued to the worshippers in this psalm which guide us in our corporate gatherings.

The first three commands are grouped by the theme of joyful worship of the king—to shout, to worship, and to come. *"Shout joyfully"* literally means to raise a joyful shout. PSALM 98:4 exclaims, *"Shout joyfully to the LORD, all the earth; Break forth and sing for joy and sing praises."* This shout refers to the shout given to a king who has just seated himself upon his throne in his capital city to the delight of his people. Yahweh is the Great King over all the earth— *"The world is Mine, and all it contains"* (PSALM 50:12). So, PSALM 100 begins with a clap of thunderous joy. It ought to reflect how we feel about our King who reigns.

The second command says, *"Serve the Lord with gladness."* We serve God with our worship as v. 4 accentuates later in the psalm. DEUTERONOMY 10:12 exhorts, *"... fear the LORD your God, to walk in all His ways and love Him, and to serve the LORD your God with all your heart and with all your soul."*

We call ourselves "servants of the Lord," and we have come into His presence to serve him. The service we render to God should be done with gladness. We do not bring honor to God when we serve with long faces and unhappy hearts.

The third command is, "Come before His presence with joyful singing." This refers to entrance into the sanctuary and into the very presence of God. PSALM 95:6 adds, "Come, let us worship and bow down, Let us kneel before the LORD our Maker." In worship we are to remember that we are now in His presence. So, this speaks of a time of formal worship—formal, yet joyful. Worshippers are regularly to come before Him in public services to magnify God's name. We assemble in His presence to exalt the greatest Being in the universe.

The fourth command tells us we should know the God we worship (v. 3). Our worship must be with the deepest personal conviction; so, it must be the product of knowing God. ACTS 17 tells us the Athenians had an altar built to "an unknown god." We must be different in our worship. We must know whom we worship. Worship that drums up the emotions and bypasses the mind does not honor a God who is so great all the words in the dictionary could not explain Him.

Three things we should know as we worship. First, "The Lord Himself is God." In PSALM 46:10 Yahweh says, "Cease striving and know that I am God; I will be exalted among the nations, I will be exalted in the earth." Second, "He made us and not we ourselves." This speaks to His power and privilege compared with our weakness and inability. It communicates effectively our accountability to God. Third, "We are His people and the sheep of his pasture." Yahweh, the King, is the Shepherd of Israel. When you come to worship, you should know God has intimate care for you because you are His sheep. In JOHN 10:14 Jesus states, "I am the good shepherd, and I know My own and My own know Me."

In v. 4, the fifth through the seventh commands serve simply to intensify the call to worship. Fifth, *"Enter His gates with thanksgiving and His courts with praise."* Gates were the front gates through which the worshippers came expecting to worship the Lord. The fact that the gates are open to us is cause enough for praise and thanksgiving. The courts were the courts of the temple—a large enclosure that could fit many thousands of worshippers. As we enter the gates and into the courts, we are to give thanks and praise. Sixth, *"Give thanks to Him."* Worshippers should have a constant mindset of gratitude, not of complaining or griping. HEBREWS 13:15 says, *"Through Him then, let us continually offer up a sacrifice of praise to God, that is, the fruit of lips that give thanks to His name."* Seventh, *"Bless his name"* (v. 4). The Hebrew term "bless" is *barak*, a word pronouncing success or prosperity or longevity on the one being blessed. To bless God is to count Him as valuable and acknowledge His enduring greatness. We ought to bless His name!

So, let us ascribe honor to God in our times of corporate worship! Do not raise an applause for the singers' and musicians' talent or performance. Bless God for His excellent name!

As you bless Him consider the greatness of His character. Verse 5 is the climax for the psalm and the basis for all the commands given previously. We worship God because He is good, loving, and faithful. Who is like the Lord in faithful lovingkindness?

Discussion & Application

1. Why does God call for corporate worship by His people and not just individual devotions and prayer?

_____

_____

_____

_____

2. What attitudes and actions should God's people bring to the time of church worship each Sunday?

_____

_____

_____

_____

_____

3. How can you or your family better prepare for corporate worship?

_____

_____

_____

_____

_____

Key Terms/Phrases

Corporate Worship = worship when the saints gather to lift up and praise His name

God-centered Worship = worship services truly focused on God's greatness, goodness, and saving acts

Yahweh = the covenant name for God in the Hebrew Old Testament which speaks of God's self-existence

Bless His Name = the name of God speaks of who He is; we are to speak well of His name in worship

Further Exploration

1 Corinthians 12 & 14; Psalm 95; 96; 149; 150;
Ephesians 2:19–22

Suggested Memory Verse

PSALM 100:4 *"Enter His gates with thanksgiving and His courts with praise. Give thanks to Him, bless His name."*

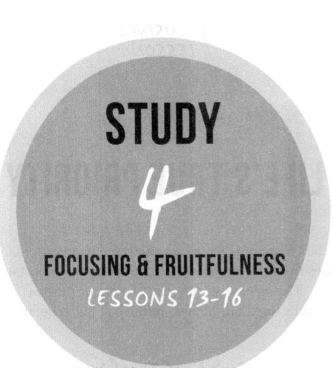

STUDY

4

FOCUSING & FRUITFULNESS
LESSONS 13-16

LIFE'S TRUE PRIORITY

> The tyranny of the urgent can force us to order our
> lives from the less important to the more important.
> That is unwise! We must keep our time in
> God's word our highest priority in our schedule!

Scriptural Teaching

LUKE 10:42B ... for Mary has chosen the good part, which shall not be taken away from her.

Many experts these days tout effective time-management, and scheduling gurus present their formulas for success. Choosing from among the myriad of scheduling systems and to-do tools can be daunting and confusing.

For the Christian, though, there is but one key that unlocks a lifetime of wise time-management. It is the key to getting the most out of your time and being the most productive for the kingdom of God. No one who desires to be productive wants to blow his time, but without this one key, that is exactly what hardworking people do every day—waste their time.

What is this key? What unlocks God's wisdom for life in every situation? It's found illustrated in Scripture in LUKE

10:38–42, and it is learned through three scenes in a true account in Jesus' life. We will take time to unveil each scene and consider this amazing key to time management.

Scene One: The Coming (v. 38)

In this first scene we see the Lord Jesus and His disciples traveling up a dusty road toward a little town in Judah called Bethany. When the Lord traveled, He usually relied on the hospitality of people in each town to provide for His ministry. His traveling core group typically needed a place to rest, to eat, to wash, and to get warm on dank and cold days.

To their delight, on this trip to Judah, a hard-working, gracious, and hospitable woman named Martha immediately and warmly welcomed Jesus and His disciples into her home. Martha's home was no skimpy Motel 6, either. She did her best to provide the Lord and His travelers with 5-star accommodations. She got busy making the preparations for all the guests with whatever comforts she could offer. (It's great to know people like this who serve the Lord enthusiastically.)

What a responsible woman and gracious hostess! Everyone must have thought well of her. She was the kind of woman who had her act together—a true model for younger aspiring women of her culture! Or was she?

Scene Two: The Complaint (vv. 39,40)

In the next scene, Jesus and the disciples have already moved inside her home and have gathered in the main room where Jesus is doing what He did best—teaching. He was a traveling Rabbi with committed students, and this home had just become His place of instruction on Jesus' favorite teaching topic—the kingdom of God.

Meanwhile, Martha is described as distracted with all her preparations. Literally Luke writes that Martha was "drawn away with all her service." Verse 39 indicates that she had a sister called Mary who lived with her, but Mary was not helping serve. Instead, Mary, while seated at Jesus' feet, was listening to the Lord's word. She had joined the group of learners who were prioritizing listening to the word of God. She believed that was the time to listen to the teaching of Christ, not to serve.

However, to Martha, Mary appeared idle and irresponsible. At first Martha may have excused Mary since she knew Mary liked to learn, but Mary just kept sitting there while Martha kept serving. Mary never jumped up to help. This neglect to help began to gnaw at Martha. In Martha's view, since Mary lived in that house too, she had a responsibility to help with the serving. How else were the people to be fed and the house to be kept clean and orderly?

So during this time, Martha became upset, not just with Mary, but with Jesus. After all, Jesus could not have missed seeing Mary sitting idle while Martha scurried back and forth tackling one chore after another. The contrast was evident to Martha, and it clearly seemed unfair to her. So at some point, Martha could not contain herself anymore. She blurted out in front of everyone, "Lord, *do You not care that my sister has left me to do all the serving alone?*" Then she went on, (and I paraphrase) "If You do care, and this is only an oversight on Your part, then tell her to help me." Her concern and question had turned into something that sounded more like a demand. Martha wanted fairness from Christ. "Shouldn't the Lord know better?" she thought. Whatever joy Martha originally had in her service had evaporated because of this perceived injustice and neglect. Her confrontation of this unfair situation now becomes the focal point of the story.

Scene Three: The Correction (vv. 41–42)

Here we reach the climax of the account, and we learn a lesson about priorities. With Martha's question/demand fresh off her lips, all eyes were staring at Martha wondering at her boldness, and then glancing back at Jesus to see how He would respond. These "tough spots" the Lord was put in at various times in His ministry served only to bring out His matchless wisdom. Our Lord has a storehouse of practical wisdom, and because of this incident we get to learn a critical part of it.

The Lord, in His amazing understanding, did not respond the way you or I might have responded. We might have leveled Martha with a sharp correction for interrupting the lesson or possibly might have made a quick capitulation, not wanting a confrontation. Jesus did neither. He spoke gently and with tender love, because He detected that Martha felt neglected, but also lacked understanding. She needed both reassurance and mild correction. At first His words and tone consoled as He began to answer, *"Martha, Martha, you are worried and bothered about many things"* (v. 41). Jesus knew her mind had been pulled away, distracted, and bothered by the needed work and service. Her attention had become dominated by the need to get things done and the responsibility which fell on her due to Mary's perceived idleness.

Jesus went on, *"But only one thing is necessary"* (v. 42). This is where the lesson becomes so helpful to us for ordering our priorities. This is where the lesson was brought to the fore. Many details and responsibilities are always there in life. Life is filled with them. Throughout life people will always weigh you down with their expectations on your time. And if you let them, those things will draw you away and consume your thinking and energy. Only one thing, though, in your life, Martha, is needed. One thing stands above the other things. One thing must be the priority when you make choices about your use of time.

What was the one necessary thing Jesus referred to? Jesus went on: *"For Mary has chosen the good part which shall not be taken away from her."* The word *"For"* connects *"the good part"* that Mary had chosen to the one necessary thing. Like Martha, Mary made a decision that day too. Unlike Martha,

Mary had chosen the good part. Mary chose the one necessary thing! *Listening to the word of God being taught with an open, receptive heart is the one necessary thing in life.* Jesus said so; and Mary chose it. Mary focused her eyes and ears fully on Jesus and prioritized the time of the teaching of God's word above other useful things. She did not let anything else, no matter how demanding, distract her from hearing the word of God carefully. She wanted to hear the Master Teacher and hear Him so well that she got up close and sat literally at His feet. That was Mary's better choice!

Making Application: The Lord commended that choice. Jesus told Martha, *"Mary has chosen the good part."* In other words, Mary has made the better choice with her time. Mary, without saying a word, becomes the silent example in the story to each of us. Her choice—to resist doing the expedient, to refuse to give in to the demands others placed on her time, even to be willing to be criticized for not doing something that someone else was counting on her to do—that silent example sitting at the feet of Jesus speaks definitively to us about our priorities. The Tyranny of the Urgent must bow to thoughtful time given to absorbing the treasured word of God!! It must be subjugated to the greater part which is listening to the word of God daily.

Let us restate that lesson: God's word is the one priority in our lives. Period! It is better, more useful, and more productive to quiet one's heart in reflection upon God's word and His plan for our lives than to do anything else in your day! It is even better to listen to the Lord's word than to serve the Lord as Martha was doing. That does not mean that all day long one just sits there and listens to the word of God and never gets up and obeys. It does mean we make absorbing Scripture the highest priority of our day and week. We should not make it an add-on when there is time, but build our schedule around it.

We have to work at this. There are 24 hours in our day, and somehow, we Christians, tell ourselves that we do not have 30 minutes (1/48 th of our day) to spend completely alone with the Lord in His word and in prayer. Let us not lie to ourselves! Time is not the problem. Making God's word a true priority is our problem.

We too have to make a choice. We have to decide what the priority in life will be. Will we make the better choice? This one choice, though not solving all your time-management conundrums, will order the rest of your life. For from the word of God flows wisdom for all life.

Discussion & Application

1. What are the main obstacles to your consistent time listening to God's word each day?

_____

_____

_____

_____

_____

2. What needs to be corrected in your thinking to persuade you to take your devotional goals this year seriously?

_____

_____

_____

_____

_____

3. What plan do you have for reading and pondering the word of God each day?

_____

_____

_____

_____

Key Terms/Phrases

Priority = the item most important to accomplish in the schedule

Correction = truth brought to another to teach him/her how to change for the better

Tyranny of the Urgent = constant demands which rule over the lives of too many believers keeping them from God's priority

Further Exploration

Deuteronomy 8:3; Psalm 63; Psalm 119; Luke 11:28; John 7:46; 8:2; Colossians 3:16.

MEDITATION: A SERMON TO YOUR SOUL

One important way to focus on the word of God is to speak it regularly to ourselves throughout the day by the blessed practice of biblical meditation.

Scriptural Teaching

PSALM 1:2 expresses that the godly man *"meditates day and night"* in God's law. The Hebrew term translated "meditates," *hagah,* is also used in Psalm 63:6, *"When I remember You on my bed, I meditate on You in the night watches ..."* Again it is used in Psalm 77:12, *"I will meditate on all Your work and muse on Your deeds."* These and other verses teach that those who wanted to live godly lives practiced meditation.

Many in our age of busyness and constant stimuli do not understand the practice of stillness and meditation very well. Those who do practice meditation often confuse it with Eastern practices. Even a good number of Christians think meditation is more about deep relaxation and focusing upon a peaceful beach scene or a soothing waterfall than focusing on Scripture's teaching.

Eastern religion uses meditation to empty the mind of all worries and personal pursuits in order to achieve harmony and oneness with nature. However, that is not what biblical meditation is about, and that inferior kind of meditation does not result in the power of God unleashed in our lives! At best, Eastern meditation tactics are relaxation techniques, and at worst, they can lead the mind into false religious experiences. For whenever the mind is turned away from biblical truth, it always wanders into error.

Nevertheless, meditation is a powerful tool given to us by God if it is done correctly. So we need to understand meditation as God intended it.

Meditation, in the Hebrew and biblical sense, is not emptying the mind or distracting the mind with beautiful sounds of nature. It is not about a body position, stretching, or drawing power from nature's energy. Meditation is focusing the mind and soul on blessed revealed truth, and then speaking that life-transforming truth confidently to our souls.

Literally in Hebrew *hagah* means "to mutter or to make a noise." The noise the Hebrews would make was the speaking of the Law of God to themselves so that they could remember it, keep it, honor God, and be blessed by it. They would memorize Scripture, repeat it to themselves, and rejoice in its warnings and promises. For that truth from God gave them guidance! The light of the law was a lamp to their feet and a light to their path (PSALM 119:105).

For us, as believers in Jesus, meditation has an important role, too. Again, it's not about sitting down, getting quiet, crossing our legs, and letting someone massage our head or play music of chirping birds while aroma wafts through the room. That may relax the body, but it does not have the power of God's Holy Spirit to transform us into Christlikeness. Really, that kind of meditation is a cheap substitute which cannot excite your soul or make you holy and godly.

Instead, meditation taps into the amazing power in the word of God. For it puts God's truth deep into the soul. There is divine energy at work when we bite into the authoritative word of God, so to speak. We chew it, savor its taste, and then absorb its words of eternal life into our being. That's real, powerful, deep-impact meditation which pushes out our old thoughts and replaces them with new divine thoughts. When a born-again child of God dedicates himself to contemplate deeply the helpful truths of Scripture, his entire being will be flooded with energy, vitality, love, peace, and joy! He will be flooded with the fruit of the Spirit (GALATIANS 5:22–23).

When scriptural truths about God's greatness and Christ's love grip your mind as a believer, those very truths excite and direct your soul into more victorious living. COLOSSIANS 3:16 exhorts, "*Let the word of Christ richly dwell within you, with all wisdom teaching and admonishing one another with psalms and hymns and spiritual songs, singing with thankfulness in your hearts to God.*" God's words, carefully contemplated and even sung, guide you and keep you from error. PSALM 119:11 says, "*Your word I have treasured in my heart, that I may not sin against You.*"

So meditation is biblical and a divine strategy to grow in faith more effectively. It goes beyond a typical twenty-minute morning devotion that only takes a bite or two of food for thought. I am not minimizing the importance of your daily devotions. Your devotions get the mind started in the right direction, but you need more truth if your mind is going to feed on the word of God throughout day. You need to preach yourself a sermon wherever you go and whoever you face.

Meditation is that sermon to self. It thoughtfully speaks Scripture to yourself so that in each area of your life, in each relationship, and in each stewardship responsibility you may respond as Christ would want you to respond—wisely, worshipfully, and thoroughly informed by Scripture. PSALM 1:2, which we read above, expresses to all believers what God instructed Joshua in JOSHUA

1:8 when He said, *"This book of the law shall not depart from your mouth, but you shall meditate on it day and night, so that you may be careful to do according to all that is written in it; for then you will make your way prosperous, and then you will have success."*

One of the reasons biblical meditation is such a catalyst to our sanctification is that the mind itself is crucial to the Christian walk. As the mind goes, so goes the rest of our Christian lives. So it matters enormously what we pay attention to throughout our day and week.

If you don't believe in the importance of your mindset, just take inventory about what tends to dominate your thinking throughout the day. For example, are you watching business reports all week while going light on time reading Scripture? Your focus likely will become materialistic rather than spiritual. Are you entertained with movies and internet games multiple times throughout the week, yet you give the Lord's word only token time? It will show up in the poverty of your spiritual life. Are you reading style magazines more than Scriptural books? You push away eternal things as you become engrossed in earthly vanity. I think you get the point. As your thoughts go, so goes your Christian life.

When Scripture is your companion all day, you are blessed in all you do; for it speaks to you of the One who is Your Lord and Friend. Scripture is focused on God and His work. So a focus on Scripture brings with it a focus on the Lord Jesus.

This focus can be with you in every circumstance of life. When stuck in traffic, you can rehearse spiritual blessings and take time to thank God for all He has done for you. When you are in a tough meeting, you can remember the wisdom of God and ask Him to bestow it upon you. When you walk outside and lift your eyes to the clouds, you can remember the promise of Jesus' coming in the clouds with power. When you gaze at a plant in the garden, you can remind yourself that your life comes from Christ and must take root in the word of God. When you overhear a foul word, you remember that bad company corrupts good morals. When the children disobey, you rehearse patience and self-control. When you work on your budget, you know God will supply all your needs.

In each and every circumstance of life you can bring God's word into focus and meditate on truth day and night. Like PSALM 119:97–100 expresses, "*O how I love Your law! It is my meditation all the day. Your commandments make me wiser than my enemies, For they are ever mine. I have more insight than all my teachers, For Your testimonies are my meditation. I understand more than the aged, Because I have observed Your precepts.*"

A godly man does not pore over the books and philosophies of unbelievers. He does not fill his mind with their articles, blogs, or opinions. A godly man wants to know how God views current events, not how the unsaved talking heads interpret life. He funnels life through Scripture, because Scripture is brilliant. Scripture is coherent. Scripture is the mind of the eternal God who knows everything there is to know. Therefore, he wants his mind thinking like God's mind does—at least as much as is possible for a mere creature.

Blessed is the man who pores over Scripture and pours Scripture into his heart. Blessed is the man who preaches himself a sermon from God's word every day!

Discussion & Application

1. In what circumstances or settings of life do you most need to start bringing God's word to mind and meditating?

_____

_____

_____

_____

2. Why is it important in some situations to speak the word of God to yourself out loud?

_____

_____

_____

_____

3. What Bible verses or passages will you choose to begin pondering this very day?

_____

_____

_____

Key Terms/Phrases

Meditation = the practice of thinking deeply on God's word for personal application

Sermon = an organized presentation of God's word through which God speaks to a congregation or person

Christlikeness = the quality or characteristic of living like Jesus lived morally and religiously

The Holy Spirit = *the third Person of the Divine Trinity who works His power in believers as they meditate on Scripture*

Scripture = *the divinely inspired infallible writings given to provide truth and knowledge of divine things*

Further Exploration

Psalm 19:14; 63:6; 77:12; 104:34; 145:5; Proverbs 15:28; Romans 6:11; 8:18; 2 Timothy 2:7; Hebrews 10:24

FRUITFULNESS THROUGH FULFILLING THE GREAT COMMISSION

> Christians are to work together to fulfill Jesus' Great Commission, advance the witness of the church to the world, and thereby be abundantly fruitful for the Kingdom of God in this age.

Scriptural Teaching

MATTHEW 28:18–20 *"And Jesus came up and spoke to them, saying, "All authority has been given to Me in heaven and on earth. Go therefore and make disciples of all the nations, baptizing them in the name of the Father and the Son and the Holy Spirit, teaching them to observe all that I commanded you; and lo, I am with you always, even to the end of the age.""*

Every Christian is a part of Jesus' church, and every believer should want to help fulfill God's purpose for the church. The church was left on earth to carry out the Great Commission.

Unfortunately, not enough Christians take the Great Commission seriously, and some do not even know what it is.

What is the Great Commission? The Great Commission was a final charge Jesus gave to His disciples right before He ascended into heaven. He charged them to take the good news of His resurrection to the ends of the earth and make disciples of all the nations. He commanded them to take the gospel from Jerusalem out to all the nations, to baptize believers, and to teach them how to be faithful disciples. As the risen Lord, He had all authority and power to command this of all His disciples. So it remains our charge today even after 2000 years of church history.

The key action and only imperative in the Great Commission passage is *"make disciples"* in v. 19. A disciple is one who is under the authority of Christ and obedient to His teachings. A disciple of Jesus rejects his own life to gain new life in Christ. A disciple is a true follower and imitator of Christ who is willing to sacrifice for Christ and follow Him all the days of his life.

How is the Great Commission to be accomplished? There are <u>three words</u> that connect to that one command and express how to accomplish the commission. These three ingredients in the Great Commission are "going," "baptizing," and "teaching." Each of these words furnishes us with more information about how to make disciples.

The first ingredient is "going." The word "go" is not technically a command in Greek. Literally the sentence reads, "having gone, therefore, make disciples of all the nations." So the going is assumed, but it is still essential to the process. Disciples who love Christ have to go to unbelievers, or at least they have to help others to carry the message to new areas. The church has to venture out to the world if she is going to reach the people who need to hear about Christ. Only this way will Jesus' church advance.

Christ knew this, and He commanded that we make disciples of all the nations, not just some of them. Though Jesus
was Jewish, He was not just pro-Israel. In fact, He was telling
His 100%-Jewish disciples that their mission would not stop at
the borders of their beloved country. It would start in Israel,
but then it would go out to all the Gentile nations. ACTS 1:8
confirms this commission because there Jesus told them that
they would be His witnesses first in Jerusalem, then Judea and
Samaria, and then to the ends of the earth. Jesus also taught in
MATTHEW 24:14, "*This gospel of the kingdom shall be preached
in the whole world as a testimony to all the nations, and then the
end will come.*" The good news of the victory of the Jewish King
and His offer of peace and forgiveness is to be proclaimed to all
people groups on the planet.

Preaching the Gospel is part of the process of going. MARK
16:15 adds, "*Go into all the world and preach the gospel to all
creation.*" In LUKE 24:47 Jesus said, "*… repentance for forgiveness of sins would be proclaimed in His name to all the nations,
beginning from Jerusalem.*" ROMANS 10:17 also instructs, "*So
faith comes from hearing, and hearing by the word of Christ.*" For
people to become disciples of Jesus, they must believe in Jesus.
To believe, they must hear the gospel message. To hear the message, the church must preach the word, proclaim the gospel, and
witness about Christ.

The Book of Acts chronicles this preaching of the gospel
from Jerusalem outward and the start of many local churches
in a wide geographical range. Those who believed the preaching
were gathered into local churches where the process of making disciples continued. For us in modern times, preaching can
include sermons on Sundays as people come to church to hear
the word. It can include preaching on the streets or anywhere
people will listen. It can be teaching in the classroom, passing
out written literature, or using the radio waves, the internet,
and TV. It can just involve talking with the people around you or

passing out written material. However, it is clear that we must take the message to the people and not sit around in church and wait for them to come to us.

The second ingredient is "baptizing." The term "baptize" used in this verse literally means, "to submerge, immerse, or dunk something." Christian baptism is the public immersion of a believer into water as a profession of his/her faith in Jesus Christ. A person who has heard the gospel, then believed it, now should be immediately baptized. Baptism is the symbol of the new believer's initiation into the life as a disciple. Notice Jesus did not indicate that this ritual was optional to the discipleship process. He declared that all authority was His, so make disciples, baptizing them. Baptism is required, not for salvation (which is by faith alone in Christ) but for proper obedience to the Lord of our salvation.

The order to follow in baptism has important meaning, too. First a person must believe, then should be baptized. This order was followed in ACTS 2:38 at the beginning of the church when Peter preached repentance followed by water baptism. This order was also followed by John the Baptist and Jesus in their baptism ministries. (See MATTHEW 3 and JOHN 1 & 3). To be baptized before believing detracts from the important symbolism of baptism, which is to profess one's faith to the world as one whose old life has now died, has been buried with Christ, and is raised (up out of the water) to newness of life. As a believer, your baptism declares to the world that your sins are washed away, and you now identify as a follower of Jesus.

The third ingredient to disciple-making is "teaching." The newly baptized believers are to be gathered in the church to learn more of Christ and His teachings. "Teaching" is the Greek verb *didask*. It means to instruct with doctrine. MATTHEW 4:23 indicates, *"Jesus was going throughout all Galilee, teaching in their synagogues ..."* That's the same word used in MATTHEW 28. It is instruction about truth from God's word. After the Sermon on the Mount in MATTHEW 7:28–29, Matthew records, *"When Jesus had finished these words, the crowds were amazed at His teaching."* Again, that is the same word.

Doctrinal teaching of objective truth from Scripture is necessary to make disciples. Notice, we make disciples not just by teaching people how to believe in Christ, but by teaching them "to observe" what Christ commanded. When we teach people, it is not merely to inform them or entertain them. It is to convince them of truth to such an extent that it leads to obedience of Christ's commandments. The church has an authoritative declaration to make on behalf of the One who has *"all authority ... in heaven and on earth."* All Jesus taught is to be learned and obeyed. The New Testament encompasses Christ's teaching, and we are to be taught to keep all of it. Jesus made it perfectly clear that teaching, and lots of it, is essential to Christianity and to be a disciple.

The early church obeyed this Great Commission. Their obedience resulted in the multiplication of disciples and local churches in the first century. Through obedience to the Great Commission we also will see God's word spread, disciples made, and spiritual fruitfulness increased. May we be dedicated to this holy task!

Discussion & Application

1. Where are you presently witnessing your Christian faith? Who are you trying to tell about Christ?

_____

_____

_____

_____

_____

2. What parts of the Gospel do you need to study more to ensure you are a stronger witness?

_____

_____

_____

3. How can you emphasize teaching more in your making of disciples?

_____

_____

_____

_____

Further Exploration

Acts 2:40; 4:17–22; 13:46; 14:5–7l 17:16ff; 1 Peter 3:15; 1 John 1:1–4; Jude 22–23; Revelation 1:5–7

16

FRUITFULNESS THROUGH SERVICE IN CHURCH

In light of Christ's soon return to earth, we should dedicate ourselves to labor in love for the advancement of the church, our brethren in Christ.

Scriptural Teaching

1 PETER 4:7–10 "The end of all things is near; therefore, be of sound judgment and sober spirit for the purpose of prayer. Above all, keep fervent in your love for one another, because love covers a multitude of sins. Be hospitable to one another without complaint. As each one has received a special gift, employ it in serving one another as good stewards of the manifold grace of God."

"The end of all things is near [at hand]." What an incredible statement for Peter to make here in his first epistle! It is the kind of declaration meant to arrest the reader's attention and focus presently on important priorities. What end does Peter mean? The end of *"all things"* he writes. In fact, *"all things"* stands emphatically forward in the Greek sentence. An emphatic

unqualified statement like this is designed to be inclusive, not limiting. All things are coming to an end. Peter, of course, is referring to the present world system—life as we know it. The verb *"is at hand"* means it has come upon us, it is within reach, and has already drawn very close.

Ponder that truth for a moment! That blessed reality should impact the way you and I think about ourselves, our time, and the use of our talents. The impending arrival of Christ is not the time to sit idly on the sidelines and wait to serve the church! All that really matters in this age is what we render to God in love, worship, and service. We must understand the times in which we live. Sense the urgency to Peter's call for service.

In the verses that follow, four actions are urged in light of Christ soon coming.

The First Action: Verse 7 says to *"be of sound judgment and sober spirit for the purpose of prayer."* Sound judgment means, "be in your right mind," "be prudent." In this context it means to weigh everything in your life carefully. Do not be sensational about events, but do not doubt either. Know about what is going on around you, and respond properly. Being *"sober of spirit"* means, "Do not be spiritually intoxicated;" "Do not be dull to the spiritual realities around you." Be alert and be aware!

Both these mindsets are emphasized in relation to an attitude that is to be maintained in prayer. *"For the purpose of prayer"* literally refers to "prayers" (in the plural). In other words, this is an attitude to carry into your prayer time. Prayer is not a lesser church activity. It is at the very heart of the church's ministry. Clear thinking about spiritual realities opens the channels for ardent and confident praying. Please notice that prayer here is not viewed as a chore to check off each day, but a privilege to unleash the power of God in your ministry. Where there is little prayer, there may be much church activity, but there will be little effective work for God. The times we live in before His coming are evil. A sober spirit fits the reality of evil and the judgment of God about to fall on the world. Bring that seriousness into your times of prayers, and you will be more productive and fruitful.

The Second Action: Verse 8 says, *"Above all keep fervent in your love for one another."* *"Above all"* accentuates this exhortation as being of prime importance. Love of the brethren is a high priority that increases our fruitfulness for God. Love drives forward much of our work in church. We are to *"keep fervent"* in our love. "Fervent" means "stretched out to full capacity; constant and intense love." This was a word used of a horse strained at full gallop or an athlete pressing his body to the maximum. This illustrates how we are to be in our love for one another. We are members of each other in the church. We were designed to work together. We must fervently care for each other. It's that simple, yet that demanding! Loving each other requires we remove the focus from ourselves and become concerned with the welfare of other believers. It is central to what we do as a church. We come together to love each other, to meet needs, to volunteer, and to help and sacrifice.

The Third Action: Verse 9 says, *"Be hospitable toward one another."* Hospitality is one concrete way to demonstrate mutual love. ROMANS 12:13 also links love with hospitality: *"... contributing to the needs of the saints, practicing hospitality."* The word "hospitable" means "one who has an affectionate concern for strangers." Hospitality offers other brothers and sisters in Christ food and shelter, room and board. Often in that day, church members would travel from one place to another and would need a safe place to stay. It was far better in that society to spend the night in someone's home than in an inn where there was often drunkenness, open sin, and danger. Hospitality met a real need for the saints.

Brotherly love shown in hospitality tied the churches together as a larger family who served each other. Missionary work was enhanced by the display of hospitality. The joy of hospitality is participating in the work of the Lord through someone else. It increases your spiritual fruitfulness because of the way you enhance someone else's ministry. Peter adds that all this hospitality should be done "without complaint." When you open your home for ministry, that can be inconvenient and costly. However, complaining about your sacrifice ruins the recipient's enjoyment of your hospitality.

The Fourth Action: Verse 10 says, *"As each one has received a special gift employ it in serving one another."* This gift refers to a ministry gift, or as it is described in 1 CORINTHIANS 12, a spiritual gift. Every believer has a gift to serve in the body. In 1 CORINTHIANS 12:7 it explains, *"But to each one is given the manifestation of the Spirit for the common good."* That is why it is vital that every believer serves the body of Jesus in some capacity. Everyone is gifted. Everyone is needed. There are no useless members in the body of Christ. Each one has already been equipped to minister to others. All believers are part of the body and are outfitted to serve in the body.

We are to *"employ it in serving one another."* The service is to build each other up in the church so that God's purposes in this world are advanced. By the ministry of spiritual gifts in love, the congregation of believers grows and matures.

Discussion & Application

1. Why is serving Christ in church an urgent and important matter?

_____

_____

_____

_____

2. How are you demonstrating fervent love for the brethren in your church?

_____

_____

_____

_____

3. How are you using your gift in service at church?

_____

_____

_____

_____

4. How can you use your home to serve the church?

_____

_____

_____

_____

Further Exploration

Acts 2:42f; Romans 12:1f; 1 Corinthians 12:1f; Ephesians 4:11–16; Titus 3:14; 3 John 5–8

STUDY

5

FAILURE & FORGIVENESS

LESSONS 17-20

17

CONFESSION BRINGS CLEANSING

When we truly agree with God about the wickedness of our sin, we please God and receive His complete forgiveness and His cleansing effect in our lives.

Scriptural Teaching

1 JOHN 1:8–10 "If we say that we have no sin, we are deceiving ourselves and the truth is not in us. If we confess our sins, He is faithful and righteous to forgive us our sins and to cleanse us from all unrighteousness. If we say that we have not sinned, we make Him a liar and His word is not in us."

Here in John's first epistle, this aged apostle makes a powerful contrast between the confession and the denial of sin. We read of two similar claims people might make in vv. 8 and 10. In v. 8 the claim is *"we have no sin."* John was pointing out that a certain group was claiming that they had no sin. In other words, they did not think they had a sinful disposition, a natural propensity to sin, or a sin nature.

That was quite a radical claim! Who made that audacious claim in the early church? John does not specify who he is referring to. However, the claim is consistent with the Gnostics whose early teachings the apostle John was opposing in this very letter. The Gnostics, who infiltrated the Christian church in the second century, claimed to have no evil in themselves. Similar to other Greek philosophies, they believed that their souls were pure and that their physical bodies were only prison houses for the human soul. They taught that their souls, through initiation rites, had fellowship with God even though in their bodies they lived a debauched and fleshly life. So they did not think that how they lived in their bodies had any bearing on their relationship with God. In other words, no matter what evil their body did, it did not adversely affect their souls, which would eventually make their way back to God. So John probably had the false teaching of these pre-Gnostics in mind.

The second claim is brought out in v. 10, "*we have not sinned*." Here the claim is similar, but it has a different emphasis. The Gnostics were also claiming that none of their actions were sinful. In their minds, they were doing only good. They believed there was nothing for them to feel sorry about or repent from. They had not sinned. Only their bodies had sinned, but it was not actually them. Not only did they not have a sinful nature, but their actions were also pure. Again that is a startling claim— one the Holy Spirit and common sense reject.

John next points out to anyone who claimed sinlessness that there are four consequences. The false claim reveals four things about them.

First, "*we are deceiving ourselves*" (v. 8): People who deny their sin are fooling themselves. They are not fooling God, obviously. He knows that we are all sinners. Our sin has not escaped His notice. He is fully aware of our propensity toward evil. However, they are leading themselves astray.

Second, *"the truth is not in us"* **(v. 8):** John was not simply writing that those people did not speak truth. He meant more than that. He was pointing out that God's truth, the gospel, the message from God, Christ Himself, was not in people who do not confess that they are sinners.

Third, *"we make Him a liar"* **(v. 10):** This statement needs to be handled with care. Since none of us can actually turn God into a liar, this means people are calling God a liar when they claim sinlessness. TITUS 1:2 declares that God cannot lie, yet some were calling God a liar because He affirms that we are sinners (ROMANS 3:10,23). If God clearly points out that all humanity is in sin and practices sin, then to claim sinlessness is to make God a liar.

Fourth, *"His word is not in us"* **(v. 10):** This means that the word of the gospel is not at all in the person who claims not to sin. This is a clear test to know if someone is saved. Anyone who denies personal sin could have never accepted the gospel of Jesus, which is predicated on a confession of personal sin and guilt. The person who denies sinful action is unsaved and unregenerate. The person who does not confess sin does not have the life of God or the word of God in his life.

These consequences are severe. One should ponder them carefully. Denial of sin has devastating eternal consequences.

Are there groups of people who deny their sin today? In what ways do people deny their sin now? Not too many people I know go around boldly declaring that they have never sinned. Some are audacious enough! They are the fools who are easy to spot. However, many deny their own sinfulness in more subtle ways. While some admit the fact of sin in their lives, they deny the guilt or responsibility for their sin. Sin to some modern "enlightened" Americans has been redefined. Sin is thought to be more like a harmless imperfection than a damning offense to a holy God. In some cases, sin is described as a virtue, not even an imperfection. For example, food is complimented as "sinfully delicious." Something that is exciting is called "wicked."

Examples of the relabeling of sin in our society abound! You may have to think about the issue a bit differently, but there are a plethora of examples. Here's one: The unbelieving world calls people who often indulge in alcohol "alcoholics," and blames the practice on a disease. Though alcoholism clearly affects the body adversely and is an addiction, God calls those who practice it something different. He calls them "drunkards" and "fools" who would never have had an addiction, or the ailments associated with drunkenness, if they had listened to His word and controlled themselves. God's labels of our sin place the moral responsibility and the burden on the individual person. The individual is required to make good choices and not dismiss his responsibility by labeling his problem a mere disease.

Here are some other examples: The unbelieving world calls same-sex relations an alternative lifestyle. God calls it a perversion of his wonderful gift of sex. Man labels discordant families as dysfunctional homes. God calls them sinful communications and actions. What man calls workaholism, God calls a love of money or pride in self-accomplishment. Man declares a person codependent. God draws attention to the person's lust for approval or even the fear of man. Man tells himself that he has an eating disorder. God commands him to repent of gluttony (if he eats too much) and to exercise discipline. Man confesses he has a sexual disorder. God calls him immoral and unfaithful. Man declares that his problem is his environment. God says his problem is his tainted heart.

So people have a way of appearing to confess sin, but not really owning up to it. They downplay it and excuse it. They have not come to grips with how wicked their hearts are and how much God loathes their sinful actions and motives. They do not believe they are worthy of the wrath of God or liable to the judgment of God. So in essence they are saying, "I have no bad sin. I only have the good and excusable kind of sin.' This is very dangerous because it is tricky. It indicates someone who is outside the realm of God's forgiveness and blessing. They will remain without forgiveness and be unclean until they admit their personal violation of the moral standards of God and their responsibility in the act.

That is the warning. Now, notice that sandwiched between these two false claims in vv. 8 and 10 is the positive sign of a person who has fellowship with God in v. 9. He is one who confesses his sin.

The concept of "confession" has been greatly misunderstood. Many folks suppose that confession involves a weekly trip to a confessional booth where a priest listens to a series of admissions. "Forgive me, Father, for I have sinned," they recite. Then some of them go out and practice the sin all over again. However, ritualistic obedience or insincere words is not what the God of truth desires. The Greek word translated "confess" here, *homologe*, has the basic meaning of "agreement." Literally it means, "to say the same things as" someone else. Confession then means to agree with God about your spiritual condition and sin. It is more than an outward statement; it refers to inward agreement that results in an outward verbal confession. What comes out of the mouth is an expression of what is truly in the heart.

A true confession would go something like this, "You are right God! I am a sinner! Since I am a sinner, I deserve your punishment. What I have done is wrong, and there is no excuse for it. I am coming to you for pardon and cleansing. I know I am weak, but I don't want to practice this ugly habit again." Since the verb "confess" is in the present tense in v. 9, the emphasis in the Greek language is that a true Christian will be one who regularly practices confession. It is not a one-time admission of guilt. It is an ongoing practice because, unfortunately, our sin is ongoing. The confessor is known as one who agrees with God about his sin. It is what he does! He does not typically try to hide his sin, but he brings it into the open and thoroughly admits it. He is not one who practices denying wrongdoing. He owns up to his part in the moral failure.

The promise to the one who confesses sin regularly and sincerely comes next in v. 9, *"God is faithful and righteous to forgive us ... and cleanse us ..."* God will cleanse the humble, confessing believer from every kind of sin. There is no kind of sin that God's power cannot forgive and cleanse. God will forgive not only the penalty of our sin, which is forgiveness, but also He will cleanse away the practice of sin in ever increasing ways as we walk with Him in the light. There is no sin, no habit, no attitude that God's power, mediated by the Spirit of God and the word of God, based on the precious blood of Jesus, cannot change. Praise be to our merciful and forgiving Lord above!

Therefore, let us confess sin like this and receive much needed forgiveness and cleansing. Let us make this our habit so that we may draw close to God. He is faithful and accepts us back in love each time we stray from His path and indulge in selfish pursuits. Let us draw courage from this promise and know that the Lord is faithful and righteous to forgive us and to cleanse us from our sin!

Discussion & Application

1. What is the meaning of confession, and how often should a Christian do it?

_____

_____

_____

_____

_____

2. How does your practice of confession need to improve?

_____

_____

_____

_____

3. What are some things you do to give the appearance of confession without really wanting to change the sin habit?

Key Terms/Phrases

Confession = agreeing with God about our sin and speaking it honestly to Him and others.

The Truth = the message of the gospel; God's declarations which conform to reality

Cleansing = the washing away of sinful practice in our lives as we confess sin and walk in the light

Further Exploration

1 Chronicles 21:8; Psalm 32; Psalm 38:18; 41:4; Psalm 51; Proverbs 28:13; Luke 15:21; 18:13; James 5:16

FORSAKING SIN IS SPIRITUALLY HEALTHY

We need to learn from the painful times we
have tried to hide our sin, and then forsake it
sooner as we trust in God's mercy.

Scriptural Teaching

PSALM 32:3–7 *"When I kept silent about my sin, my body
wasted away Through my groaning all day long. For day
and night Your hand was heavy upon me; My vitality was
drained away as with the fever heat of summer. Selah. I
acknowledged my sin to You, And my iniquity I did not hide;
I said, "I will confess my transgressions to the LORD"; And
You forgave the guilt of my sin. Selah. Therefore, let everyone
who is godly pray to You in a time when You may be found;
Surely in a flood of great waters they will not reach him. You
are my hiding place; You preserve me from trouble; You sur-
round me with songs of deliverance."*

Second Samuel 11 and 12 inform us that when King David
came to power in Jerusalem, he lusted after Bathsheba from the

rooftop of his palace after spotting her bathing. The problem
was that Bathsheba was not his wife. With this evil, adulterous
desire in his heart, he then summoned Bathsheba to the palace,
committed adultery with her, sent her back home, found out
that he got her pregnant, then tried to cover up the whole mess
by having Uriah her husband sent to the front lines to be killed
in battle. This was a great sin for a man who had previously
walked so closely with God.

David, though, did not disclose his sin to anyone. Like so
many people today, he chose to hide his sin rather than confess
it. The pain David experienced by hiding his sin is seen and felt
in vv. 3–4. These verses reveal the deceit in David's heart. He
did not want anyone to know what he had done. He did not even
confess it to God. Instead he began a process of self-justification
and rationalization. He covered it up.

Yet, David knew what the law of God declared, "*Thou shalt
not commit adultery; Thou shalt not murder.*" His conscience
could not be settled so easily while his sin was shouting so loudly
within. His mouth was quiet about his own sin, but his conscience screamed. In this state of internal civil war, he became
a silent mourner.

David continued to play religion, but he also continued to
carry the knowledge of his unconfessed sin in his conscience
all the day long. When writing this psalm, he vividly remem-
bered how a lack of confession tortured him. He wrote in v.
3, "*My body wasted away through my groaning all day long.*"
Literally it means "my bones," "the frame of my body." The
strongest portion became weak. The more he tried not to confess, the more his conscience yelled. So he groaned and roared
on the inside. Verse 4 says, "*Day and night Thy hand was heavy
upon me.*" He did not confess, so he got no rest. He felt this
constant inner pressure and pain. Not even nighttime brought
relief, for thoughts of his sin dogged him during his dreams and
made him lie in bed awake for hours at a time. Much of this was

the pressure of conscience, but God added heavier and more severe pressure to the normal working of the conscience. Thus David experienced not communion with God, but His chastening displeasure.

Unconfessed sin can literally destroy a person—soul and body. The last part of v. 4 says, *"My vitality was drained as with the fever heat of summer."* Literally it means his life's juices were turned into the drought of summer. It was as if the summer heat of sin burned down upon him and dried up his vitality. His problem was not psychological, as many would describe it today. It was spiritual. It had to do with his relationship with God. Pills and therapy do not fix that kind of pain. If we sin, and we try to hide it from the church, we may hope God will ignore it, but God will not ignore sin. God is willing to forgive confessed sin but not ignore it. Expecting Him to wink at sin is foolish.

If there is sin festering in your heart, you are not dealing honestly with it. The Spirit of God is grieved by your cover-up. Joy escapes you as you sense the heavy hand of God's displeasure upon you. That heavy weight is designed to force you to your knees, end the silence, and bring out the heartfelt and humble confession.

Notice the sharp contrast in v. 5 that shows the benefit of confessing and forsaking sin. Verse 3 says, *"I kept silent."* Verse 5 says, *"I acknowledged."* At last David spoke! Verse 5 is the heart of the Psalm. Here David makes his confession, and what a turnaround has occurred! Pain has turned into relief. Gloom has turned into joy. Notice the whole confession is personal and relational toward God. *"I acknowledged my sin to Thee."* *"And my iniquity I did not hide."* He knew his sin was primarily a sin against God. As he wrote in Psalm 51, *"Against Thee, Thee only have I sinned and done what is evil in your sight."*

David gave no mere intimation of having "sort of sinned," but gave a full explanation of his guilt. Verse 5 is only the summary of his confession. Psalm 51 is the full and detailed confession itself. In this confession he did not feel self-pity. He knew he deserved the pain he was receiving. If you suffer under sin and have self-pity, you are not confessing. You are actually blaming God for being so hard on you. There are no excuses in genuine confession. David let God's mercy be God's mercy. He wrote in v. 5b, *"You forgave the guilt of my sin."* All of it was forgiven! It was immediate forgiveness never to be brought up again. David confessed it all, and God forgave it all. *"I did not hide my iniquity."* That means I uncovered my iniquity, and You covered it.

PROVERBS 28:13 says, *"He who conceals his transgressions will not prosper, but he who confesses and forsakes them will find compassion."* Confession should go hand-in-hand with forsaking sin. Confession clears the air between you and God. Confession reveals that you want to be true in your relationship with God.

Therefore, sin not confessed and not forsaken is a great obstacle in the way of greater fellowship with God. You cannot get around sin. God will not let you. The more you grow in Christ, the more He will make you deal with your sin honestly. JAMES 4:7 tells us, *"Draw near to God and He will draw near to you. Cleanse your hands you sinners and purify your hearts, you double-minded."*

Discussion & Application

1. What does unconfessed sin do to a believer?

_____

_____

_____

_____

_____

2. Describe the relief and joy of forgiven sin.

_____

_____

_____

_____

3. Why is important to join confession with the forsaking of sin?

_____

_____

_____

4. Do you have unconfessed sin which you need to uncover now?

_____

_____

_____

Key Terms/Phrases

Concealment = covering up sin when it should be confessed openly to offended parties and then forsaken

Conscience = inner part of man wherein he passes judgment on his attitudes and actions

Transgressions = sins against God where we violate His stated and revealed will

Further Exploration

Read all of Psalm 51 and make observations about confession.

Also read the rest of Psalm 32 and see how stubbornness keeps us from learning the lessons God wants us to.

FORGIVING: HOW OFTEN?
LESSON

UNLIMITED FORGIVENESS

Christ's command to offer unlimited forgiveness to others is surely hard, but it is God's will and something we must ask God's strength to carry out.

Scriptural Teaching

MATTHEW 18:21–22 *"Then Peter came and said to Him, 'Lord, how often shall my brother sin against me and I forgive him? Up to seven times?' Jesus said to him, 'I do not say to you, up to seven times, but up to seventy times seven.'"*

Both the Old and New Testaments teach us that the one true and living God is abundant in forgiveness. PSALM 86:5 declares, *"For You, Lord, are good, and ready to forgive, and abundant in lovingkindness to all who call upon You."* God demonstrates great forgiveness. God also demands forgiveness from us towards others. LEVITICUS 19:18 says, *"You shall not take vengeance, nor bear any grudge against the sons of your people, but you shall love your neighbor as yourself; I am the LORD."* In COLOSSIANS 3:13 we read,*"… bearing with one another, and forgiving each other, whoever has a complaint against anyone; just as the Lord forgave you, so also should you."*

Forgiveness is hard, let's admit it! Look again at MATTHEW 18:21. This section starts with Peter's question to Jesus. The context reveals that Peter was listening to the Lord speak about sin. He was thinking about what the Lord was teaching. He knew there were wicked people out there who would purposefully take advantage of others. Plus, their offenses could grow worse over time. Forgiveness would seem weak and vulnerable to these opportunistic sharks. It probably seemed to Peter that if you chose the path of forgiveness, like Jesus was teaching, you were opening yourself up to harm. People would cut you up into little pieces and devour you if you kept forgiving them.

So Peter stepped forward to ask an appropriate question of Jesus: *"How many times should I forgive my brother?"* If I may paraphrase his intent, it might sound something like this: "If you forgive someone over and over, won't they just keep doing wrong and taking advantage of you? Isn't forgiveness even an incentive for them to continue to wrong you? When are we allowed to get back at them?" Many are fearful that in an ongoing dispute, if they give in first (such as in a marriage struggle) they will appear as the weaker of the two. To Peter's credit, he personalized the question. He was not asking an abstract philosophical question about forgiveness. He was anticipating what would happen in his relationships if he obeyed Christ's teaching. He looked down the road and anticipated how hard it would be to forgive. So he asked Jesus, *"How many times?"*

Do you know why this is a great question? It is great because we all know forgiving others is hard. Oh, yes, we know it from personal experience. Every one of us has been wronged by others. Sometimes the wrongs have been vicious and unrelenting. The only defense we seem to have is to hide or fight back. Because it is so difficult, Peter's real question to the Lord was does forgiveness have limits? And if it does not, who can actually fulfill limitless forgiveness?

The only way to answer this question is to think about God's forgiveness of us. EPHESIANS 1:7 says, *"In Him we have redemption through His blood, the forgiveness of our trespasses, according to the riches of His grace."* In ACTS 10:43 we read, *"Of [Jesus] all the prophets bear witness that through His name everyone who believes in Him receives forgiveness of sins."* God's forgiveness of all our sins was clearly not selfish. The purpose for God's forgiveness was not so that God could feel good about Himself. God already felt good about Himself because He is perfect. Forgiveness was a purely selfless act. In the case of humans, the power to forgive others comes from the realization of our own forgiveness. From the humbling we experience by having our sins wiped away comes the will to offer forgiveness to others. God wants us to learn love, so He first loves us. God wants us properly motivated, so He has us experience the power of His forgiveness as the prerequisite for forgiving others. He does not tell us to forgive others to achieve inner peace or nirvana! He tells us to forgive because we were forgiven.

Consider the great example of Christ on the cross. He emptied himself for us! Sure, there are those who forgive in order to manipulate others at some time in the future. "I'll forgive you, but then you owe me one," is the motive. They view forgiveness as a weapon to use against people in the future. This kind of forgiveness just moves the debt owed from one bank account to another. The debt is not actually forgiven; it is still owed. That's not real forgiveness. Real forgiveness is much more thorough and much harder.

The rabbis of Jesus' day had an answer for the quantity of forgiveness question. Jewish tradition gave this answer: Three times. They got that idea from a misunderstanding of verses like AMOS 1:3 which says, *"Thus says the LORD, 'For three transgressions of Damascus and for four I will not revoke its punishment ...'"* They reasoned that God punished after three offenses, so they should be allowed to also. So they did better than the "three strikes and you're out" law. They said four strikes and you are out. Believe it or not, that was more merciful than other civilizations, some of which frowned upon mercy altogether.

Peter did even better with his answer. Peter wanted to demonstrate how magnanimous his heart was. He knew Jesus was more gracious than the self-righteous Pharisees. So as a disciple of Jesus, he was willing to forgive up to seven times! Forgiving once was hard, twice was harder, but to forgive the same person seven times indicated a huge heart! Peter must have thought he was standing on firm moral ground.

Jesus' answer shocked his sandals off his feet! In v. 22 Jesus declared that forgiveness was to be unlimited: *"Do not forgive seven times, but forgive seventy times seven."*

Did you start doing a multiplication problem in your head to find out the limit? Don't bother! This answer went so far beyond anything in their minds. This they had never heard before. This must have seemed crazy to them, honestly. Of course, the number was not to be taken literally. It was not to end even at 490 times. It was obviously meant to heighten the amount to the unlimited category. "Forgive them on and on" is the meaning. There are to be no limits to forgiveness because there are no limits to God's forgiveness of you. Jesus might have been purposefully echoing GENESIS 4:24 where in the pre-Flood earth Lamech boasted, *"If Cain is avenged sevenfold, then Lamech seventy-sevenfold."* In other words, Jesus was taking Lamech's boast of dealing out great revenge and reversing it and transforming it into a standard of dealing out great forgiveness. Do not be great in revenge; be great in granting pardon.

Surely this is a supreme challenge to our hearts that we cannot fulfill by our own power. We are too selfish in heart to offer this kind of pardon for others. Yet there it stands written. And here we are humbled before God, needing to lean on Him totally to have the humility and graciousness of our God. May God increase our love toward our fellow man as we rejoice in

His forgiveness of us! May we begin this day to forgive others
who have wronged us.

Discussion & Application

1. Do you have someone you need to forgive right now? What
will you do?

_____

_____

_____

2. Have you ever had to rely upon the Lord's strength to forgive
someone multiple times? How did you feel?

_____

_____

_____

3. Why is important to forgive others as Jesus said?

_____

_____

_____

Key Terms/Phrases

Forgiveness = removal of the debt owed to you as an expression
of love to the debtor

Vengeance = taking justice into your own hands and exacting
retribution on others who have offended you

Offense = an action or word by another which causes you pain
or sorrow or loss

Further Exploration

Exodus 34:7; Psalm 99:8; Luke 6:37; 11:4; 17:3; 23:34;
Ephesians 1:7; 4:32; Colossians 1:14

FRUIT: LOVE:
LESSON

20

THE PREEMINENCE OF LOVE

Love is imperative in the body of Christ; it is more important than the most skilled spiritual gifts working within the church. Really!

Scriptural Teaching

1 CORINTHIANS 13:1–3 "If I speak with the tongues of men and of angels, but do not have love, I have become a noisy gong or a clanging cymbal. If I have the gift of prophecy, and know all mysteries and all knowledge; and if I have all faith, so as to remove mountains, but do not have love, I am nothing. And if I give all my possessions to feed the poor, and if I surrender my body to be burned, but do not have love, it profits me nothing."

Chapter 13 of 1 Corinthians has been called "the Love Chapter." What some people forget is that it is set in the context of Paul's teaching about using spiritual gifts in the church for the edification of the body of Christ. The chapter seems at first as if it is dealing with a new topic, but it is not an entire break from the theme of spiritual gifts. Spiritual gifts are the topic in the chapter before and after, so the teaching on love is supportive and complementary truth introduced to help the Corinthian church understand how to use spiritual gifts in love. Unfortunately, the Corinthians had let their zeal for spiritual gifts produce pride in themselves and thus overshadow love for others in the body.

Love, however, is the weightier responsibility of the believer. Love is the necessary light that makes the spiritual gifts glow with God's glory. So before resuming his teaching on spiritual gifts in chapter 14, Paul first sees the need to explain the right attitude or atmosphere in which the gifts of the Spirit must operate in a local church. The fruit of the Spirit—namely love—must characterize the use of the gifts of the Spirit.

In the opening three verses of the chapter, Paul compares the value of love to four different super-gifts of the Spirit. He writes of these gifts in a hypothetical extreme just to show that, even in their greatest possible manifestation, they pale in comparison to love. Love is always greater. The comparison Paul makes is not an actual one, of course. No one actually has the super-gifts he proposes in these verses. Instead Paul exaggerates the gifts to prove a point to the Corinthians. In effect, he is arguing a case. Love necessarily goes with the gifts, or the gifts have no value in God's church.

First, Paul hypothetically creates a speaking gift of tongues so great it surpassed anything the Corinthians knew. He describes a person with total spiritual giftedness speaking all tongues of men and angels, but who is utterly void of the Spirit's fruit of love. How great would this person be as an asset to the church? The second half of the verse tells us how a super linguist would be valued in the church if he spoke without love: "*I have become a noisy gong or a clanging symbol.*" A noisy gong was just a piece of bronze without musical ability. It reverberated loudly and was unpleasant to the ears. You would not want your home located near some obnoxious instrument like that. A clanging symbol was most likely a concave shaped metal plate used in pagan worship. We are told it had a rather repelling sound. So a person without love is just a noisy irritant and an aggravation to the eardrum. He is so preoccupied with his grand giftedness that he is oblivious to the needs of others. It does not matter that a speaker can keep people spellbound with his or her oratory abilities. No one even wants to listen to someone speak who speaks without love.

Second, Paul zeroes in on those who would exalt the gift of prophecy, the gift of knowledge, and the gift of faith in v. 2: "... *and if I have the gift of prophecy, and know all mysteries and all knowledge; and if I have all faith so as to remove mountains, but do not have love ...*" According to chapter 14 prophecy exceeded tongues for usefulness toward the church. It was one of the greater gifts. So how would having the gift of prophecy stack up if you had it to such an extent that you knew all things? Please note how impressive a gift Paul is postulating. It means full mastery of the Bible coupled with absolute knowledge of every area of theology. Before he answers that question, Paul adds another impressive gift. *"If I had all faith so as to remove mountains ..."* This person could say, "Be picked up, Mt. Everest, and be thrown into the Indian Ocean." This person would have no shortage of confidence in the power and promises of God. He would be so believing of every word of God that he could do even great miracles of nature, and such great miracles that not even all the apostles put together performed. What if a person had faith like that? Right now you might be thinking, "Who cares about love if you got that kind of a gift? Let's be practical! This guy would be a phenom!" That's not what God thinks. God gives His estimate of a man like this: *"I am nothing."* In God's estimation, there is nothing in that person to esteem.

Third, the comparison of personal sacrifice without love comes in v. 3. *"And if I give all my possessions to feed the poor and deliver my body to be burned but have not love ...."* This may seem like a strange comparison. After all, who would have the gift of giving and make sacrifices for the poor without love? Yet that is exactly what Paul is describing. This is benevolence without love; charity without care. It is sacrifice without selfless love. The giving is more about the giver than the one getting the gift. This person is giving away all he has, but not being satisfied, he even delivers his own body to be burned. That completes the hyperbole. What benefit would this giver have? *"It profits me nothing."* When sacrifice is driven by self-interest and a desire for status, it forfeits all its spiritual value.

With these three comparisons, Paul has closed his case! The loveless person produces nothing of value, is nothing of value, and gains nothing of value. This makes a powerful point. Love is pre-eminent to have and express. Believers in church should pursue love before anything else. In any ministry they are a part of, they should be striving to use it to care for people. Preaching without love is nothing. Serving without love is nothing. Giving without love is nothing. Love is *that* important. Love is that essential!

Obviously this calls for each of us to grow in love and express sincere love to one another. We should stress a humble practice of love not show off our abilities. We should seek to build others up not elevate ourselves. Any Christian service not bathed in the practice of love is detrimental to the body of Christ.

Discussion & Application

1. How does 1 Corinthians 13 impact your thinking about the importance of love?

_____

_____

_____

_____

_____

2. In your personal spiritual goals, how much does love for others drive forward your commitment to your goals?

_____

_____

_____

3. In what specific ways do you think you need to show more love within the body of Christ?

_____

_____

_____

Key Terms/Phrases

Love = the great attribute of God He instills in us to care for the needs of others before ourselves

Spiritual Gift = abilities given to each Christian by the Holy Spirit at the time of salvation to serve in the body of Christ effectively

Further Exploration

1 Corinthians 16:14; Galatians 5:6,13; Ephesians 4:2,15; 5:2; Philippians 1:9; 1 John 3:11,14,16,23; 4:7–11

STUDY

6

FORTIFYING FOR
SPIRITUAL WARFARE

LESSONS 21-24

CHRISTIAN, YOU ARE IN A SPIRITUAL WAR

As a Christian, whether you realize it or not, you have entered a spiritual war. Therefore, you must be sober and vigilant in spiritual battle.

Scriptural Teaching

EPHESIANS 6:10–11 *"Finally, be strong in the Lord and in the strength of His might. Put on the full armor of God, so that you will be able to stand firm against the schemes of the devil."*

These verses in Ephesians teach that the church of Christ is involved in a conflict. It's a real war with eternal consequences. It would be foolish, therefore, for Christians to enter this battle casually—neither understanding their weapons nor being aware of their opponent's tactics.

When most people think of spiritual warfare, they think of scary things like demonic possession and exorcism. The truth is that most spiritual battles occur in everyday temptations and circumstances of life. The events of life often are the result of the fiery missiles of the evil strategist who exploits any Christian who is a poorly prepared soldier of the cross. In fact, the more you grow in Christ, the more intensely you can expect the battle to rage around you. In the words of the Apostle Paul, "... *all who desire to live godly in Christ Jesus will be persecuted*" (2 TIMOTHY 3:12).

Put aside "bad luck" as the explanation for the strange opposition to your Christian life. The world is not run by magic charms or lucky stars. Let us not be naive! As sure as God exists, there is a spirit world. For God Himself, according to JOHN 4:24, is spirit. Not all those spirits out there are working in your favor. So, spiritual warfare is not simply an exciting topic to discuss. It is a reality for which you as a Christian should prepare.

These two verses serve as Paul's trumpet blast rallying the believing troops to action. The blast begins with the word, *"Finally."* Paul means, "Finally, here at the close of this letter to the Ephesians, where we have covered the church's tremendous privileges in Christ and responsibilities in the world, I have this final charge on spiritual warfare to bring this epistle to a worthy close." That charge is this: *"Be strong in the Lord and the strength of His might."* Paul's overall goal in chapters 1–3 of EPHESIANS was to get the church to understand the incredible privileges and powers available to believers in Jesus Christ. The letter's second purpose is accomplished largely in chapters 4–6. Paul urges the church to be responsible to use those God-given resources to walk worthy of its Christian calling. Those two purposes come together in Paul's final charge in v. 10: *"Finally, be strong* [that's our responsibility] *in the Lord and in the strength of His might* [that's His resources!]."

So this must be an important command for believers. *"Be strong"* in the Greek is the Greek verb *endunamousth.* It is a present passive imperative. Literally it commands, "Be continually made strong in the Lord." That means the Christian cannot be strong in the battle on his own. He is doomed to lose if he thinks that way. It's the Lord's power that fortifies the believer.

So soldiers of Christ arise! This is a call for valor! The trumpet is blasted to prepare you for battle. Much like the call to Joshua in JOSHUA 1:9 where he was about to enter the land and face great opposition, but he needed to know who would really win the battle: *"Have I not commanded you? Be strong and courageous! Do not tremble or be dismayed, for the Lord your God is with you wherever you go."* Similarly, we cannot enter this spiritual war relying on our own strength.

How then do we appropriate and use this amazing power of God in battle? Verse 11 teaches that we will first have to *"Put on the full armor of God."* "Put on the full armor of God" is the explanation of how to be strong in the strength of the Lord's might. In other words, you'd better not be like that excited rookie soldier who hears the reveille call in the morning and excitedly rushes out of his tent into the battle without preparation. We have to go into the battle *"in the strength of His might"* or we do not stand a chance of victory. The armor of God is essential to the battle.

There are **six things** Paul explains here about putting on God's armor:

First, this is not a suggestion but a command. To disobey this command will result in harm to you.

Second, the very fact that he is commanding Christians to put on the armor of God means that the armor is already available to us. It is not something we have to go out and get or ask God to provide. We don't pray for the armor. We just need to put it on.

Third, we are responsible to put on the armor. We are not passive in this process. We must take an active and deliberate role in putting on the armor. God does not put it on for us.

Fourth, it is described as the armor *"of God."* That means it comes from God, and it is carefully crafted to give you victory in battle. You will not find better equipment for spiritual battle. God is the best outfitter of equipment. So trust His skill and craft.

Fifth, the full armor is needed not just one or two items. Some believers might want to go skimpy on the equipment. That would not be wise. The Christian soldier must be protected from head to foot. The inexperienced soldier leaves one or two pieces behind only to be wounded in battle and learn the hard way.

Sixth, this armor is not just for a special crisis but for the duration of the Christian life. The verb indicates a one-time putting on and leaving on. So pick it up, put it on, and leave it on. That is the idea!

We will pick up with this thought in our next lesson.

Discussion & Application

1. Why do you think it is important for Paul to wake us up with a trumpet blast and make us aware of the spiritual battle?

_____

_____

_____

_____

2. What place does strength and valor have in living the Christian life?

_____

_____

_____

_____

3. How can you appropriate God's power?

_____

_____

_____

_____

4. How do you go about putting the armor of God on and then leaving it on?

_____

_____

_____

_____

Key Terms/Phrases

Spiritual battle = conflict which wages in spiritual places including ideas, temptations, and teachings

Armor of God = the protective spiritual equipment to allow the believer to stand his ground against spiritual attacks from the enemy.

Power of God = God's energy available to the believer as he wears and uses the armor of God

Further Exploration

1 Samuel 17:47; Romans 13:12; 1 Corinthians 16:13;
2 Corinthians 10:4; 1 Timothy 6:12; 2 Timothy 2:1; 4:7

FORTIFYING:
LESSON

WHY YOU MUST FIGHT THE BATTLE, PART 1

The Christian must fight the spiritual battle
because he has relentless and formidable spiritual
foes opposed to his progress in faith.

Scriptural Teaching

EPHESIANS 6:11–13 *"Put on the full armor of God, so that you
will be able to stand firm against the schemes of the devil.
For our struggle is not against flesh and blood, but against
the rulers, against the powers, against the world forces of
this darkness, against the spiritual forces of wickedness in
the heavenly places. Therefore, take up the full armor of God,
so that you will be able to resist in the evil day, and having
done everything, to stand firm."*

Here Paul provides reasons for spiritual warfare in EPHESIANS
6:11b–13.

The first reason we need the full armor of God is because we
have a formidable enemy. Notice in v. 11 the little word *"that"*—
"that you may be able to stand firm." The Christian prepares

because he has an enemy who wants to send him running from the battle hiding, cowering, and surrendering. Inherent in this command to stand firm against the schemes of the devil is that the attacks of Satan are real, formidable, and certain.

If you are not strong in the Lord by putting on the full armor of God, you will not be able to stand firm even if you are a Christian. You're going to get scared! You're going to get confused! You're going to get tired and weak! You will respond unwisely! You will back up, and you will run in retreat! That does not honor your Captain Jesus Christ who put you into the battle to win and have a positive spiritual impact on others.

In the Christian walk there will be moments where you will have to stand your ground against the enemy. Verse 13 exhorts, *"Take up the full armor of God that you may be able to resist in the evil day."* There is some debate concerning what Paul meant by *"the evil day."* With the double use of the article in Greek it is clearly referring to a specific day. Back in 5:16 Paul wrote that the days we live in are evil, but the way this is worded, it points to a particular evil day. Some see in this a reference to the last day, a time in which Satan has his evil way. That is possible from the grammar, but the context does not support this interpretation. The end times are not in view in EPHESIANS 6. The urgency of the preparation for these Ephesian Christians, along with the very personal image of wrestling in v. 12, indicates that this evil day is that day when Satan and his forces will choose to target each Christian or church. Unknown to us because these things are decided in spiritual places, there is a critical time of assault when Satan's forces move against each Christian and each church. Even in the case of Jesus Christ, the 40th day of His fasting in the wilderness when He became hungry was Satan's target day. Satan came to Jesus in a powerful way on that day and attacked Him with three choice temptations. However, the Lord Jesus was prepared. He stood His ground. It was Satan who fled Jesus, not the other way around. Jesus is a great Captain to learn from and follow.

That is why we need the armor of God too, so we can stand firm when Satan attacks. Three times Paul writes *"stand firm"* (vv. 11, 13, and 14). Christians must stand their ground on that evil day when Satan comes at us with particularly strong temptations.

What does a Christian look like who stands firm against the devil?

First, he is not frightened by the devil. When the assault comes, if the Christian gets afraid, he has lost the battle already. Scared soldiers do not usually stand strong. They flee!

Second, it means he does not droop or slouch at his post. He does his duty with vigor. *"Fight the good fight of faith,"* Paul writes in 2 TIMOTHY 4:7.

Third, the Christian does not even think about retreating. We must be resolute to meet the enemy head on and not flee.

Fourth, he will always be on the alert. A sentry half-sleep at his post is ill-prepared when the attack comes. We are taught in 1 CORINTHIANS 16:13, *"Be on the alert, stand firm in the faith, act like men, be strong."*

Notice Paul does not merely say to stand against the devil but to stand firm against the schemes of the devil. We have to stand not just against sheer power but against trickery, too. That makes the battle trickier. *"Schemes"* is the translation of the word *methadu*. These are the devil's carefully crafted battle methods or strategies. This is his X and O game strategy. These are his cunning ploys designed to catch believers off guard and ruin their joy and testimony in this world.

The devil is a master deceiver and spiritual strategist. This evil guy is #1 on the FBI most-wanted list: "Formidable, Blasphemous, Insurrectionist."

Satan is *formidable*. REVELATION 12:9 says, *"... the serpent of old, who is called the devil and Satan ... deceives the whole world* ..." The whole inhabited earth is deceived by this one spiritual being. You do not get that way without plenty of powerful schemes.

Satan is *blasphemous.* He calls people to worship him rather than God. Jesus properly responded to this temptation in MATTHEW 4:10, *"Go, Satan! For it is written, 'YOU SHALL WORSHIP THE LORD YOUR GOD AND SERVE HIM ONLY.'"*

Satan is an *insurrectionist.* He opposes everything God, the true King of the universe, does. MATTHEW 12:24–30 teaches that Satan is a king. He has a rebellious kingdom. Yet his kingdom will not prevail in the end.

Paul was not one who was unsuspecting of Satan's activities. 2 CORINTHIANS 2:11 says, *"in order that no advantage be taken of us by Satan; for we are not ignorant of his schemes."* Satan's attacks are not always direct frontal assaults. He can roar like a lion to strike fear into the believer, as Peter indicated in 1 PETER 5:8. Or he can also slither as a serpent and whisper enticing lies to the unsuspecting as we read in 2 CORINTHIANS 11:3: *"I am afraid, lest as the serpent deceived Eve by his craftiness, your minds should be led astray from the simplicity and purity of devotion to Christ."*

Discussion & Application

1. Why is it important to use the armor of God to stand first against the devil's schemes?

_____

_____

_____

_____

_____

2. What are different schemes the devil uses to hinder or hurt Christian soldiers?

_____

_____

_____

_____

_____

3. In what ways do you need more courage in the Christian battle?

_____

_____

_____

_____

Key Terms/Phrases

Satan = an evil spiritual angelic being who opposes God and leads a host of spirit beings against God's agenda and God's people

The evil day = a targeted day when evil forces strategically try to discourage, dissuade, or destroy believers

Stand firm = the military command to the believer in fighting against spiritual forces by which he does not retreat or give in to any spiritual intimidation or temptation

Further Exploration

Psalm 27:14; Matt. 4:1; Luke 22:31; John 16:33; 2 Cor. 5:6; Phil 1:14; 1 Thess. 2:18; 1 Pet. 5:8; Rev. 2:10

23

WHY YOU MUST FIGHT THE BATTLE, PART 2

Christians must fight the spiritual battle by
resisting the devil because our foes are
organized to hinder our progress.

Scriptural Teaching

EPHESIANS 6:11–13 *"Put on the full armor of God, so that you
will be able to stand firm against the schemes of the devil.
For our struggle is not against flesh and blood, but against
the rulers, against the powers, against the world forces of
this darkness, against the spiritual forces of wickedness in
the heavenly places. Therefore, take up the full armor of God,
so that you will be able to resist in the evil day, and having
done everything, to stand firm."*

The second reason we must fight the battle is that we have a
struggle against evil forces (v. 12). The little Greek word *hoti*,
translated *"For"* at the beginning of the verse, indicates that
Paul is giving an expansion of the first reason. Not only should
we rally to the battle due to the schemes of the devil, but also

because those schemes will involve struggles with all the hosts of wickedness. We are in a struggle with them whether we recognize it or not. The word *"struggle"* literally means "a wrestling."

Who is our struggle against? Notice the strong contrast in v. 12 when it says, *"not against flesh and blood, but against ..."* Paul does not mean that our wrestling is sometimes with flesh and blood and sometimes with evil spirits, but that it is not at all against flesh and blood. Feeble humanity is not the true enemy. As evil as some people act, our battle is not with them. We focus far too much on the wrongs others do to us and fail to understand what is really happening behind the scenes. One of Satan's greatest delusions today is that no unseen war rages at all. This delusion encourages us to think that all our problems are generated simply from physiological or psychological sources. We focus far too much anger and energy against other people and not against the spiritual forces behind evil. So don't be fooled!

Paul mentions **four spiritual groups** we wrestle against. Probably these four groups represent strata of organized evil spiritual beings under the leadership of the devil mentioned in v. 11. Scripture teaches that good angels are organized by rank and duty. Christ, for example, refers to legions of angels in MATTHEW 26:53. Michael is called an archangel showing his higher rank. It is reasonable to conclude that Satan's angels, true to Satan's character as a deceiver, also are organized in a mimicking fashion of God's angels. MATTHEW 12:45 speaks of some evil spirits being more wicked than others. 1 CORINTHIANS 15:24–25 also says Christ will abolish all rule, authority, and power, *"For he must reign until He has put all His enemies under His feet."* So these groups are Christ's enemies whom He currently has authority over but who are yet to be abolished.

The first evil group mentioned is *"the rulers"* (*archas*). These do not refer to political powers on earth, for earthly rulers are flesh and blood. Rather it is in the sense already mentioned in the letter—the spiritual rulers in the heavens connected with the schemes of the devil. These are demonic leaders with their particular areas of supervision and rule. These may refer to the lowest class of rulers in Satan's hierarchy.

The second group mentioned is *"the powers or authorities."* This is again a reference to demonic beings. Demons are powers. This may refer to their role in promoting paganism, the occult, and the worship of many gods. In referring to idol worship going on in ancient Greece, Rome, and Egypt, Paul writes, *"The things which the Gentiles sacrifice, they sacrifice to demons, and not to God"* (1 CORINTHIANS 10:20).

The third group in v. 12 is called *"the world forces of this darkness."* This phrase is used only here in the NT, *kosmokrat ras.* It indicates one who has might or strength over the world. The term was used in classical Greek of military conquerors. Since the darkness refers to the spiritual darkness of this world, the world forces wage war to maintain their darkened empire. Darkness defines the kingdoms of this world.

The last group we war against is called *"the spiritual forces of wickedness in the heavenly places."* This is the devil and his hordes of wicked spirits. The highest of them dwell *"in the heavenly places,"* which is the same place as *"the air"* mentioned back in EPHESIANS 2:2. Spiritual forces have a domain in heavenly places (in atmospheric places) but not in the highest heaven where God's throne is.

In these verses Paul is commanding us to stand firm and to use our armor. This stance does not involve having verbal confrontations with demons like Christ and His apostles did, and who were specially gifted and empowered in that regard. We are not to command demons in the name of the Lord Jesus. Nor must we learn some technique to figure out how to draw out the name of a demon in order to exorcise it. Nor are we to march around cities 7 times and claim the territory for Christ, as some today advocate. Nor is Paul teaching here what we frequently hear people pray, "In the name of Jesus Christ we bind Satan from working." You cannot bind Satan! Christ bound Satan as He plundered Satan's forces in the gospels. The great angel in the end times will bind Satan and shut him in the abyss as REVELATION 20 promises. We, however, are not given that authority.

Nor are we to use various rituals for exorcising demons such as crucifixes and special incantations. Notice that is not at all what Paul teaches about how to be ready for spiritual battle. We are instead to do what James says in 4:7, "*Submit therefore to God; resist the devil and he will flee from you.*" And we are to put on God's armor. Our authority is not the issue. Jesus and God have authority over the demons, and all we are responsible to do is to use the word of God to repel evil spirits. Demons run from the truth of God.

(To be continued in the next lesson.)

Discussion & Application

1. How can you begin to view your world through the lens of a spiritual battle and not just disconnected occurrences?

_____

_____

_____

_____

_____

2. Why is it wrong to try to bind Satan?

_____

_____

_____

_____

_____

3. In what ways do you think spiritual forces are hindering the work of the church?

_____

_____

_____

_____

Key Terms/Phrases

Spiritual darkness = defines the evil character of Satan's kingdom which advances lies and disobedience

Heavenly places = spiritual locations in which evil spirits are allowed to move and have their levels or areas of control and authority

Spiritual wrestling = the very close and personal activity we must engage in while resisting evil when it comes our way instigated by evil spirits

Further Exploration

Luke 11:26; Acts 8:7; Acts 19:12f; 1 Cor. 10:20–21;
1 Timothy 4:1; 1 John 4:1

FORTIFYING:
LESSON

WHY YOU MUST FIGHT THE BATTLE, PART 3

Each piece of spiritual armor is important to get the believer ready to stand firm against all the wicked spiritual forces Satan marshals against the church.

Scriptural Teaching

EPHESIANS 6:14–17 *"Stand firm therefore, having girded your loins with truth, and having put on the breastplate of righteousness, and having shod your feet with the preparation of the gospel of peace; in addition to all, taking up the shield of faith with which you will be able to extinguish all the flaming arrows of the evil one. And take the helmet of salvation, and the sword of the Spirit, which is the word of God."*

To win in a spiritual battle we must decisively take the armor of God, put it on, and leave it on. Here Paul describes 6 pieces of the believer's armor. The order Paul chooses is not random but represents a normal order a soldier equips himself.

First, the believer must be one who has *"girded his loins with truth."* In those days men wore long, loose tunics, so girding the loins was vital preparation for any vigorous activity, especially going to battle. The loose tunic had to be bound together and tucked under the leather belt so it would not get in the way during crucial maneuvers. Obviously, without this first step of preparation, the rest of the armor could not be properly fitted. Girding with truth is the first step to prepare the Christian soldier.

Truth is used both in an objective sense, as when Jesus said in His prayer to the Father, "*Your word is truth*," and in a subjective sense such as back in v. 4:25, "*speak truth with each other.*" There truth refers to our character of truthfulness. Paul likely meant truth in both senses. Only God's truth will stand against the schemes of the devil, yet His truth has to be appropriated in our lives. So to be girded with truth means to live in harmony with the truth of God's word and be truthful and genuine in all our dealings with others. We need to remove all guile and hypocrisy. We need to make sure we practice no disguises as Satan does.

One of the devil's schemes is to exploit half-hearted Christians. Satan loves pointing out anything he thinks smells of insincere motivation towards God—lethargic love towards others, indifference to the truth of God, mediocrity in service—all attract the attention of the devil whose very name means "slanderer." Another scheme of the devil is to drag people into lies. Lying opens the door for the devil to work in one's life, because the devil "*is a liar and the father of lies*" (JOHN 8:44). The devil's people live in a world of deceit! The believer speaks truth in love (v. 4:15).

The **second** piece of armor is "*the breastplate of righteousness.*" The breastplate covered the vital organs. It covered the soldier from neck to thigh often including his back. It was made of bronze, though some officers had chainmail breastplates. Like the word "*truth,*" there are two senses of righteousness meant here: Christ's righteousness imputed to us is our guarantee of acceptance with God and protects our life with God;

then we also must practice His righteousness in our daily lives. In 1 THESSALONIANS 5:8 it is called the *"breastplate of faith and love."* So it refers to an applied righteousness. To be obedient to all you know is to put on the breastplate of righteousness.

Satan has many tricks to lure believers into sin. In times of prosperity he finds it easier to lead people into materialism. Also he draws believers into self-indulgence and hedonism. "If it feels good, it must be ok with God. I will only do it this once. I just want to have the experience. I can resist another day. Besides, everybody is doing it, even some of my Christian friends." On and on go the devil's tricks. Then when he has his sport with you, he stands and accuses you before God of doing the very sin he lured you into.

The **third** piece is feet shod with the preparation of the gospel of peace. The military success of any army in those days depended not only on bravery and skill but on how well their feet were shod. For the soldier, proper footwear provided both mobility toward the battle and firmness of grip in combat. To prevent disadvantage in battle, a Roman soldier's sandals had bits of metal and jagged pieces fixed in their soles to give the needed traction in any terrain.

The Christian soldier also should shod his feet with the preparation of the gospel of peace. This does not mean (as some think) that the feet of the Christian soldier should bring the gospel of peace to others. Paul is not writing about evangelism in this context. It means that the gospel of peace is the foot's preparation. This works three ways. First, peace makes us sure of our favorable relationship with God. ROMANS 5:1 says, *"Therefore having been justified by faith, we have peace with God through our Lord Jesus Christ."* To fight spiritually you have to be sure you are right with God. Second, we are prepared by the peace that exists in our relationships as Christians. EPHESIANS 2:16–18 states, *"Christ reconciled them both in one body to God through the cross."* Satan can churn up a lot of trouble in the church by stirring up anger and hurt feelings. Peace protects against Satan's attempts at division. Third, peace prepares us by granting inner peace of mind. JOHN 16:33 says, *"These things I have spoken to you, so that in Me you might have peace. In the world you have tribulation, but take courage; I have overcome the world."* You can see why the devil hates this piece of armor. He loves confusion, disharmony, and uncertainty.

Fourth, the *thurion*, the "shield," was an oblong Roman shield 4 feet long and 2 ½ feet wide. It was constructed of wood with 2 layers of leather glued and bound together with iron above and below. It was designed to cover the whole person in a slightly bent position. When soldiers would fight side-by-side, these shields would form an impenetrable wall from oncoming arrows or from the jabs of enemy foot soldiers. In ancient warfare, arrows were occasionally dipped in tar or pitch and then ignited and shot by the thousands to rain down on enemy troops. A direct hit on a soldier could be damaging even with his other pieces of armor on. However, with the timely use of his shield, dozens of these little arrows could be rendered harmless, because when the flaming arrow hit the shield, the arrow would be embedded in the leather and wood and become severely blunted and then harmlessly extinguished. In fact, at times, Roman soldiers would even soak their shields in water just before battle if such arrows were expected from the enemy.

Obviously the shield was another important piece of armor. Notice Paul says *"in addition to all, taking up the shield of faith."* He means, "Do not neglect to pick up the shield! Your previous armor is not complete without it." What is this shield for the Christian? Faith! The shield is faith in the promises of God. No Christian can be successful apart from the daily exercise of faith. How many of the enemy's schemes would be foiled if we but exercised our faith more decisively? Satan will search for some weakness in the church circling around the shields to find someone not covered, and then he will order the barrage of arrows to come and rain down darts of discouragement and arrows of doubt.

There are many flaming arrows, but notice v. 16 says the shield will extinguish them *"all."* It puts out the darts of confusion, the missiles of doubt, and the arrows of fear flung to lodge deep within you. When you come out to the other side of a spiritual battle, you appreciate the shield of faith more. Faith becomes a valued defense.

Fifth is the helmet of salvation. *"Take the helmet of salvation"* really is a verb meaning "receive" the helmet. The picture is that of someone standing by to hand the helmet to the soldier because the shield is now in the left hand. So take the helmet, and put it on, and leave it on.

This piece of armor might seem a bit perplexing because all Christians are already saved. 1 THESSALONIANS 5:8 helps us to understand when it says, *"but since we are of the day, let us be sober, having put on the breastplate of faith and love, and as a helmet the hope of salvation."* This supplies a reasonable meaning to our Ephesians passage—future salvation—as in 1 PETER 1:5, which says, *"a salvation ready to be revealed in the last time."* Our salvation is fully guaranteed now, but it is not fully realized. It is the hope that is the helmet in battle. When soldiers in battle begin to waffle in their expectation of victory, they become weakened and feeble. This hope gives stability because it gives confidence in ultimate victory. So hope really is the anchor of our souls (HEBREWS 6:19).

The **last** piece of armor requires the most skill to use—the sword of the Spirit. The sword referred to is the *machaira*—a short sword no longer than 18 inches, or shorter. In close combat it was the main weapon of the Romans soldier. This sword was kept in its sheath and pulled out quickly for any purpose.

This is the only weapon mentioned by Paul that has the ability to meet the lunge of the enemy, beat him back, and make him flee. The sword of the Spirit means it is the Spirit's sword. It is what He uses, and it originates with Him.

The written word of God is the powerful effective sword. ZECHARIAH 4:6 says, *"'Not by might nor by power, but by my Spirit,' says the LORD of hosts."* The Holy Spirit is powerful in spiritual battle, but He will not use human swords. He will not use human might or human wit or human reason or human philosophy. Churches that promote those things have no ability to beat Satan's attacks back. The Spirit will only accomplish His work through His sword.

Did it ever occur to you that you lose some battles to sin because you do not know how to use your sword well? You have only a vague or inaccurate understanding of the Bible. That kind of use of the sword is unprofitable. Would you want to charge into battle swinging your sword wildly? Is there not a difference between a trained swordsman and an untrained one? Satan is skilled at twisting Scripture. We must be skilled at bringing out the right use of Scripture in the right situations. While Satan plans his schemes, you need to hone your sword. We do that by learning to make careful application of the Bible in our lives. We read the Bible, studying its context and exercising discernment so we can rightly apply it daily to our thinking and action. Only this kind of use of the Bible, from a believing heart, yields a skilled swordsman.

Discussion & Application

1. Why must we put on truth first in the spiritual battle?

_____

_____

_____

_____

2. How can failing to practice righteousness open up your vitals to attacks from Satan's hoards?

_____

_____

_____

_____

_____

3. What are some ways not applying the gospel of peace can invite the devil's havoc?

_____

_____

_____

_____

_____

4. Explain why the hope of salvation is so important when you are engaged in spiritual battle with the devil.

_____

_____

_____

_____

_____

5. Name a couple of practical ways you can improve in your use of the word of God?

_____

_____

_____

_____

6. How have you used faith to put out arrows of doubt or discouragement?

_____

_____

_____

_____

Key Terms/Phrases

Sword of the Spirit = the Bible, God's word, which must be used accurately and with skill to expose and beat back the lies of the devil

Truth = the truth of God and truth spoken inside of us as a guard against the lies and hypocrisies generated by evil

Righteousness = (two senses) both the right standing we receive as a gift from Christ and our practice of right living according to the commands of God. Both ward off the scheme of wickedness in our lives

Peace = the calm assurance God gives us in our hearts as we enjoy peace with him and harmony in our relationships with others

Hope = the expectation of victory every spiritual soldier needs in his fight against evil; looking forward to future salvation in all its glory

Faith = the shield which extinguishes Satan's arrows of doubt, discouragement, and despondence

Further Exploration

Eph 5:9; 1 Timothy 6:11; 2 Timothy 3:16; 2 Timothy 4:4;
Titus 1:14; 2 Peter 2:2; 1 John 3:18; 3 John 3; Col 1:23;
1 Thes. 3:2; 5:8; 2 Thes. 1:11; 1 Timothy 6:11–12;
Romans 8:24; Galatians 5:5; 1 Thes. 4:13; Hebrews 4:12

STUDY

7

FELICITY (JOY), FORBEARANCE, FUTURE HOPE & FAITHFULNESS

LESSONS 25-28

25

THE JOY OF THE LORD

Inexpressible joy in the heart of a believer is the proper response to a thoughtful contemplation of our great salvation in Christ.

Scriptural Teaching

1 PETER 1:6–8 "In this you greatly rejoice, even though now for a little while, if necessary, you have been distressed by various trials, so that the proof of your faith, being more precious than gold which is perishable, even though tested by fire, may be found to result in praise and glory and honor at the revelation of Jesus Christ; and though you have not seen Him, you love Him, and though you do not see Him now, but believe in Him, you greatly rejoice with joy inexpressible and full of glory,"

The Christian life is meant to be a joyful life. Many believers have lost sight of God's joy and no longer experience it in their lives. Yet Peter in the beginning of v. 6 starts this section with these effervescent words: *"In this you greatly rejoice ..."* There is brightness and optimism in these words. It means that in your Christian hope you greatly rejoice. The last part of v. 8 expands on that thought by asserting, *"Though you do not see* [Jesus] *now but believe in Him you greatly rejoice with joy inexpressible and full of glory."* The literal translation of *"greatly rejoice"* is that "we rejoice with joy." That verb for rejoicing is in the present tense, so it refers to continuous joy in the life of the Christian. In other words, our Christian faith gives us great cause for rejoicing through our present trials even before we see Jesus Christ in all His glory.

Why do Christians greatly rejoice in the present age though it is filled with trials? Joy is abundantly present in our hearts because we have a fantastic anticipation of what is to come. We anticipate glory and the full experience of eternal life. That glorious anticipation of what we will see and gain is churning in our hearts and minds right now! Our faith in Christ generates a joyful hope! Because we believe in Jesus now, that belief hopes for great things to come. We read of this incomparable future inheritance in 1 CORINTHIANS 2:9 which says, *"but just as it is written, 'THINGS WHICH EYE HAS NOT SEEN AND EAR HAS NOT HEARD, AND which HAVE NOT ENTERED THE HEART OF MAN, ALL THAT GOD HAS PREPARED FOR THOSE WHO LOVE HIM.'"* We have never experienced what we are going to receive, and we can hardly imagine it. We know, whatever it is, it will be so good and beyond our imagination!

Why, then, when Christians gather at church, do we often look melancholy, doleful, or filled with confusion? Believers often fail to rejoice because they have lost sight of what they believe and what it means. Peter is refocusing believers on their salvation. He is writing that joy should be the norm of our experience as we contemplate our blessed hope. As we think of Jesus and our full salvation to come, we should be rejoicing greatly.

Peter heaps on the descriptive words for this kind of joy. He writes that you rejoice with joy! No, there is even more to what he writes, *"you greatly rejoice with joy"*! That is better, but that does not even quite express it. "You greatly rejoice with joy inexpressible and full of glory"! That is what he is communicating. Wow! That kind of joy is what our belief in Jesus grants to us! The more you study your salvation and understand your future inheritance, the more your joy crescendos.

It is always a joy to hear the pastors at the Shepherd's Conference at Grace Community Church in Los Angeles each year singing with joy about their salvation. Pastors who regularly preach the word of God know their salvation better than most. True thoughts of their salvation cause exuberant expressions of joy. Yet it truly is so great it must be described as inexpressible joy! This word *"inexpressible"* occurs nowhere else in the New Testament. It means indescribable. How do I describe the joy I have because of the salvation Jesus has given me? It is ... well ... it is so deep, so gripping, so all-consuming, so satisfying. Peter writes, "I cannot describe it!"

Is that how you feel about your salvation and your future in heaven? If not, think more deeply and earnestly about what you have been given in Christ. Think about how secure it is! Think about all God gives you by His grace. Let it sink in. Then rejoice in the Holy Spirit!

Joy is a powerful state of mind. Yet it is not natural. When you rejoice in Jesus, others will look at you and will not be able to figure you out. They may wonder, "Is this guy on drugs? Did he win the lottery? Has he been healed from cancer?" God's joy has nothing to do with outward circumstances in this passing life. Our joy transcends circumstances. It is the joy of the Lord, and we are rejoicing greatly with a joy that is full of glory! Joy is not the shifting happiness that accompanies the change in external circumstances. God's joy is not the thrill of a roller coaster ride. When thrill-rides end, that kind of happiness vanishes and leaves you feeling unsatisfied. Thrills do not change the heart. They do not penetrate deeply enough. True joy is an inner power, a great outburst of inner excitement at the thought of eternal life with God. God's joy is not dependent on the changes in circumstances because there is one overriding circumstance that never changes: Jesus will win!!! And you, by faith, will be victorious with Him!

That is why Peter also writes in 1 PETER 4:12–14:

Beloved, do not be surprised at the fiery ordeal among you, which comes upon you for your testing, as though some strange thing were happening to you; but to the degree that you share the sufferings of Christ, keep on rejoicing; so that also at the revelation of His glory, you may rejoice with exultation. If you are reviled for the name of Christ, you are blessed, because the Spirit of glory and of God rests upon you.

That is why Paul writes in PHILIPPIANS 4:4, "*Rejoice in the Lord always; again I will say, rejoice!*"
PSALM 95:1–3 wonderfully exclaims:

O Come, let us sing for joy to the LORD; Let us shout joyfully to the rock of our salvation. Behold, God is my salvation, I will trust and not be afraid; For the LORD God is my strength and song, And He has become my salvation.

ISAIAH 61:10 joins the chorus with these words:

I will rejoice greatly in the LORD, My soul will exult in my God; For He has clothed me with garments of salvation, He has wrapped me with a robe of righteousness, As a bridegroom decks himself with a garland, And as a bride adorns herself with her jewels.

Present sorrows cannot weaken Christian joy. Paul testified in 2 *Corinthians* 6:10 "[that he was] *sorrowful yet always rejoicing* ...*" Peter says your faith in the promises will cause you to rejoice with a great joy, because you will receive the goal of your faith—your excellent salvation. Latch onto this hope, and nothing will be able to diminish the flame of your God-given joy!

Discussion & Application

1. Why do you think we often don't have the joy we should because of our great salvation?

_____

_____

_____

2. Do you want to experience more of the joy of the Lord? Do you really?

_____

_____

_____

3. What changes in thinking do you think would help you to have more joy?

_____

_____

_____

Key Terms/Phrases

Joy = the overwhelming attitude and emotion of godly satisfaction, optimism, excitement, and exuberance

Inexpressible = not able to be put into words because it is deep and hard to express

Further Exploration

Romans 15:13; 2 Corinthians 7:4; Galatians 5:22; 1 Thessalonians 2:19–20; Hebrews 12:2; Jude 24

26

GOD IS ABLE TO MAKE YOU PERSEVERE IN YOUR CHRISTIAN WALK

The Christian life is long and often rugged. God ensures the believer will be able to make the full journey all the way to His glorious eternal kingdom.

Scriptural Teaching

JUDE 1:24–25 *"Now to Him who is able to keep you from stumbling, and to make you stand in the presence of His glory blameless with great joy, to the only God our Savior, through Jesus Christ our Lord, be glory, majesty, dominion and authority, before all time and now and forever."*

The letter of Jude was written to those in the church who had experienced false teachers penetrating the church and leading some among them astray. These false teachers insidiously tempted those inside the church to indulge in fleshly acts. Witnessing this apostasy was unsettling to the faithful. That is why Jude not only exposed the evil of these apostates, but he ended his epistle with a strong doxology breathing hope into the hearts of believers.

Notice how the doxology begins: "*Now to Him who is able ...*" That is a basic biblical truth we need to have firmly fixed into our souls. God is able! That is something we are to know for sure. Where others cannot accomplish things, God can! Where trouble abounds, God's power abounds still more. "*Evil men and impostors will proceed from bad to worse,*" the apostle Paul warned in 2 TIMOTHY 3:13. Problems will mount, but God's solutions are measureless. Mary asked the angel "*How can I be with child if I know not a man?*" Gabriel, who stands in the presence of God, knew without hesitation, "*Nothing will be impossible with God.*" Paul wrote confidently in EPHESIANS 3:20, "[God] *is able to do exceeding abundantly beyond all we ask or think.*" So we must believe in God's ability to accomplish great things even when others are turning their backs on the gospel and walking away into a lives of worldly sin.

Here Jude specifies two things God is able to do. These are carefully chosen to fit the circumstances his readers faced. "*Now to Him who is able to keep you from stumbling and to make you stand in the presence of His glory ...*" While you face the schemes of the devil, while you try to root out the evil men in your midst (vv. 2–3), while you try to reach the lost with the gospel (vv. 22–23), God will keep you from stumbling. In other words, He will prevent you from succumbing to temptation! He will give you the strength and insight needed to stand against their intimidation and resist their appeals to the sensual flesh. With all the enticements to sin and all the subtleties of false teaching, the Lord God will sustain your faith and walk. You will not stumble so as to be eternally harmed. God will protect you and your faith!

This divine preservation of the soul finds its evidence in a doctrine the church calls "the perseverance of the saints." This doctrine simply means that all true believers maintain their faith in Christ and obedience all the way to the end of their lives. They never stumble so as to fall away from the Christian faith. MATTHEW 24:13 reflects this doctrine when it declares, "*The one who endures to the end, he shall be saved.*" FIRST CORINTHIANS 15:2 teaches that the gospel saves people "*... if you hold fast the word which I preached to you unless you believed in vain.*" HEBREWS 10:38 warns, "*If* [the professing believer] *shrinks back, My soul has no pleasure in him.*" However, then the writer to the Hebrews concludes in v. 39, "*But we are not of those who shrink back to destruction, but of those who have faith to the preserving of the soul.*"

How are believers able to persevere to the end? The true believer perseveres because of God's mighty provisions. It is not we who are able, but God who is able to do great things in and through us. God provides new life in Christ that is eternal life and cannot end. God grants the permanent indwelling of the Holy Spirit who will never leave us or forsake us. Christ constantly intercedes for His own at the right hand of the Father so no sin will be able to cut us off from God. Jesus prayed in JOHN 17:11, "*Holy Father, keep them in Your name.*" Then in v. 15 he prayed for His disciples saying, "*I do not ask You to take them out of the world, but to keep them from the evil one.*" So, we will persevere in our faith to the end because of God's keeping power. Peter also refers to God's mighty protection in 1 PETER 1:5 when he says, "*... [you] are protected by the power of God for a salvation ready to be revealed in the last time.*" As Jude says in v. 1:24, "*He is able to keep you from stumbling*" and He is able "*to make you stand in the presence of His glory.*"

Beloved, this is where the faith journey leads. This is where your walk of faith ends; when you stand in the presence of God's unimaginable glory. That promise reflects the doctrine of eternal security that states that once someone is saved by God, he can never lose that salvation. He most assuredly will be taken to glory. Eternal security reminds us to rest peacefully in the power of God. That's how secure we are in Jesus! Once He saves us, we are saved permanently. The proof is that He promises to take us all the way to glory. How great that will be when we bask in the radiance of His divine love and light, beholding His face forever! Notice Jude's contrasting imagery. Rather than stumbling, we will stand. We will stand before Him "*blameless*" without fault and with no sin on the record books. That will be a day of great and incredible joy. No one can fathom how great the joy will be when we stand before His majesty.

Both our eternal security and our need to persevere in the faith are taught in Scripture. Eternal security is taught to remind us that we were chosen in Christ before the foundation of the world (EPHESIANS 1:4). God saves us and what God starts He will complete (PHILIPPIANS 1:6)! If any of us sins, Christ intercedes on our behalf (1 JOHN 2:1). The need for perseverance is taught to show that we have responsibility to choose Christ, to walk with Him, and to remain true to Him unto the end. We may not be complacent in our spiritual journey; thus, the command to persevere. Nor may we be fearful of losing our salvation; thus, the promise of eternal security. In confidence we claim the promises of God relying on his power and protection, and then we prove His work by abiding with Christ to the end.

Discussion & Application

1. Why is the doctrine of eternal security so reassuring to the Christian?

_____

_____

_____

_____

_____

2. How do the doctrines of God's preservation and our perseverance work together?

_____

_____

_____

_____

_____

3. How have you been impacted by other supposed Christians walking away from Christ and back into the world?

_____

_____

_____

_____

_____

Key Terms/Phrases

Preserve = the work God does to safeguard our faith and protect it so that we have strength to persevere

Persevere = the quality of continuing in the Christian faith through life all the way to the end

Apostasy = the state of falling away from following God and His word; it results in destruction

Eternal security = the doctrine that teaches that once a person is truly saved, he is saved permanently; once saved, always saved.

Further Exploration

John 10:25–30; Romans 12:12; 1 Timothy 4:16; James 1:12; 1 John 2:24, 28; 2 John 9

27

A HOPE FIXED ON JESUS' SECOND COMING

Christians should fix their minds upon
their purifying hope as they wait expectantly for
the Second Advent of Jesus Christ.

Scriptural Teaching

1 JOHN 3:2–3 *"Beloved, now we are children of God, and it has not appeared as yet what we will be. We know that when He appears, we will be like Him, because we will see Him just as He is. And everyone who has this hope fixed on Him purifies himself, just as He is pure."*

1 PETER 1:13 *"Therefore, prepare your minds for action, keep sober in spirit, fix your hope completely on the grace to be brought to you at the revelation of Jesus Christ."*

Jesus is going to appear in the clouds and return bodily to earth. That is God's promise, and that has been the Christian hope for 2000 years. The passage of time does nothing to wane that hope, rather it intensifies it as we see the day drawing closer. It is a powerful hope, for it purifies the Christian as we wait for the arrival of the blessed and holy Son of God.

In the first passage above, 1 JOHN 3:2, the Greek verb for "appear" is *phanerōthē*, which means "to manifest, make plain, or appear." The verb is in the passive voice to indicate that God will reveal Christ in the sky when He comes again. This appearing refers to the glorious second appearance of Christ as opposed to His first appearance in humility veiled in human flesh. Though we firmly believe in the first coming of Jesus, and thank God for it, our hope is in the second appearing of Jesus Christ.

This hope is a superior hope to what people in the world possess today. While so many folks put their hopes in material things expressed in words like, "If I could just have that exquisite house or that fine job, or if I could just retire early or have more vacations, then everything would be alright," the Bible repeatedly makes it clear that the Christian's hope is not in things in this world but in Christ's appearance in glory. For example, in 1 TIMOTHY 1:1 it reads, *"Paul, an apostle of Christ Jesus according to the commandment of God our Savior, and of Christ Jesus, who is our hope…"* Did you catch what our hope is? Jesus Himself is our hope. We hope in the arrival of Jesus, and Jesus is pure. 1 JOHN 3:3 points out that those who wait expectantly for the Pure One to appear will purify themselves in the present. This hope purifies us because we long for the Pure One to come! Since He is pure, those who live their lives waiting for Him purify sinful elements out of their lives.

All other worldly hopes will ultimately disappoint you. Do not put your hope in things that are passing away and can never satisfy the human soul. They will leave you empty, disappointed, and without true hope. Hoping in Christ will never disappoint you, because hoping for Christ is no wishful fantasy. The term "hope" is commonly used that way these days. People exclaim things like, "I hope I do well on my test," or "I hope it doesn't rain on my picnic." That wishful thinking is not what the Bible means by hope. The Christian hope is a confident expectation that Christ will keep His promise and will reveal His glorious kingdom with all its benefits when He appears! HEBREWS 10:23 urges believers, *"Let us hold fast the confession of our hope without wavering, for He who promised is faithful."* Since God never breaks His promises, we can be certain Christ is coming.

Christian hope may be defined this way: A forward-looking faith, confidently anticipating God's blessings at Christ's return and producing assurance and purity during the present life. We look for our hope not in the stock market or the next election but in the skies. We keep our expectant eyes looking upward. TITUS 2:13 says, *"Looking for the blessed hope and the appearing of the glory of our great God and Savior, Christ Jesus."* Christ is God and Savior, and we wait for Him and no other. Peter adds that our hope is a living hope because the One we hope in is literally alive from the dead: *"Blessed be the God and Father of our Lord Jesus Christ, who according to His great mercy has caused us to be born again to a living hope through the resurrection of Jesus Christ from the dead"* (1 PETER 1:3).

There is no uncertainty about our hope, and this is why hope is such a great motivator. 1 PETER 1:13 tells us, *"Fix your hope completely on the grace to be brought to us at the revelation of Jesus Christ."* That is an explicit reference to the hope spelled out in 1 PETER 1:3–12. We are urged to hope totally in the coming grace, not in the present temporal life. *"Fix your hope"* indicates a single-minded focus of the Christian life which unfortunately not enough believers maintain. That is why Peter has to emphasize it here. None of our hope should be in this world. This world and everything in it will perish. 1 JOHN 2:17 says, *"And the world is passing away, and also its lusts; but the one who does the will of God abides forever."* All those who put their stock in this world's evil system, according to 2 THESSALONIANS 2:8, will lose. They have no real hope. That verse predicts, *"And then that lawless one [the antichrist] will be revealed whom the Lord will slay with the breath of His mouth and bring to an end by the appearance of His coming."* That is why our hope is the best hope.

Like John, Peter is not encouraging us to drown out our present trials in dreams of better days. Hope is not a pretend game. This is not religion as the opiate of the people, as communism once defamed Christianity. This is a call for a full evaluation of present lifestyle, goals, and pursuits in light of that one approaching, defining moment in history when we will see Jesus coming on the clouds with power. We have set our expectations high. Nothing less than that glorious appearance will satisfy us! Nothing less we look for!

What are you doing to be ready for that day when your hope is revealed? If Jesus were revealed today, what have you been doing that prepares for that day? How does your job fit in with that day? How does your daily routine connect with that day? How does your school preparation anticipate that day? That's the one controlling event of all other decisions in this life. Neither the ups and downs of the economy nor your business' success should govern your decisions, only Christ's coming. How is what you are doing today an expression of your hope in the coming of Jesus tomorrow? In what way are you really fixing your hope completely on the revealing of Jesus in glory?

This verse in 1 PETER 1 says there is grace to be brought to believers at that time. Beloved, this is special and wondrous truth meant especially to brighten our faces and reinforce the joy in our hearts! There is still grace from the hand of the Lord to be gained. This grace is what we long to receive. We hope for Jesus Christ. We hope for His second coming. We hope for His glorious revealing in the heavens. We hope for the grace He will bring when He is revealed in glory. There is a whole bundle of undeserved blessings coming our way when He visibly reenters human history. Stay riveted on that, and you cannot go wrong!

Discussion & Application

1. Evaluate your present circumstances in light of your hope.

_____

_____

_____

_____

2. How strong would you say your current anticipation of Jesus' arrival has become?

_____

_____

_____

_____

3. What would you be ashamed of if Jesus came back today?

_____

_____

_____

_____

Key Terms/Phrases

Hope = confident anticipation of the coming of Christ according to the promise of God

Revelation = the unveiling of Jesus in glory

Appearance = similar to revelation it means Jesus becoming manifest and plain and obvious to the world

Second coming = Jesus' second entrance into this world in obvious power and glory, unlike His first coming in humility and lowliness

Purity = the state of moral and spiritual cleanliness increased by Christian hope in the Pure One, Christ

Further Exploration

2 Corinthians 5:10; 1 Thess. 3:13; Hebrews 9:28; James 5:7–8; 2 Peter 3:4–12; 1 John 2:28; Rev. 1:17

FAITHFULNESS:
LESSON

28

REMAINING LOYAL TO CHRIST

> Since we serve a completely faithful God, believers should be loyal to God in their hearts and lives, never abandoning their faith in Christ.

Scriptural Teaching

JOHN 15:4 *"Abide in Me, and I in you. As the branch cannot bear fruit of itself unless it abides in the vine, so neither can you unless you abide in Me."*

The first part of the verse commands *"Abide in Me, and I in you."* So, abiding in Christ is clearly something important Christ wants us to do.

Some people have been taught a wrong concept of Christian abiding. Abiding is not something mystical or a deeper level of Christian living for some Christians. It is not something some Christians do, and other Christians have not yet learned to do. All true Christians abide, because abiding has to do with continuing in the Christian faith. The verb "abide," *men,* is very common and simply means "to stay put" or "to remain where you are."

A physical illustration of abiding comes from ACTS 27:31. Paul was aboard a ship that was being battered by a storm in the Mediterranean Sea. So, Paul said to the centurion and to the soldiers, "*Unless these men remain in the ship, you yourselves cannot be saved.*" The word "remain" is the same verb, and it clearly means they should not leave or abandon the ship. They must stay in the ship, stay put, or they will drown.

JOHN 8:31 uses the verb figuratively and spiritually when Jesus urges, "*If you continue in My word, then you are truly disciples of Mine ...*" Continuance in listening to and applying the word of God to your life is the mark of a true believer. It is abiding in Christ.

In the last line of v. 4, the present active verb shows that abiding is not meant as a one-time thing but something to be continual. Indeed, it is inherent in the very idea of abiding, because you cannot really stay put and then leave and call that abiding. If one left, he would not be abiding. Abiding by definition cannot be fickle. It must be steadfast and faithful.

The constancy of abiding is also obvious from the illustration in JOHN 15. A branch abiding in the vine must be continuous. Any breach from the vine results in fruitlessness and death to the limb.

Reverse abiding is also needed. Jesus also abides or remains in believers. In other words, not just believers abiding in the vine is needed, but the vine continuing to provide the juices of life to the branch. The relationship is both intimate and mutual. However, notice there is no verb in the second part of the phrase. So, it is not a command for Jesus to abide. He does not need a command. He will do His part. He is faithful to us all the time. FIRST CORINTHIANS 1:9 directly states, "*God is faithful...*" SECOND THESSALONIANS 3:3 adds, "*... the Lord is faithful, and He will strengthen and protect you from the evil one.*" So, we do not need to worry about God. He has His end secured. God is always faithful to us. It says in 2 TIMOTHY 2:13, "*If we are faithless, He remains faithful, for He cannot deny Himself.*"

Faithfulness is needed on our part because of what will happen to us if we are not faithful. The illustration of the vine and branches indicates to us that we are not a self-contained entity. As a branch separated from the supply of nourishment cannot produce fruit, neither can any of us apart from Christ. Fruit-bearing for the disciple is totally, one-hundred percent dependent on a direct vital connection to Jesus. We must remain true to Christ if we want to bear fruit and continue to receive His life juices.

Abandoning the vine is not an option for a believer. It results in drying up, being burned, and perishing. This is not meant to illustrate that someone loses his salvation; rather, not abiding proves the professing believer was never truly saved in the first place. To turn one's back on Christ is a serious offense and reveals that the person's faith was spurious all along. True believers remain believing. They continue in their loyalty to Christ, to His word, and to His kingdom to the end. They will be tested along the way, of course, and they will have bad seasons in which their faith slumps or languishes, but they will always come back to their Lord and Savior. True believers abide!

The context in which Christ spoke this parable makes clear the meaning. JOHN 15 was spoken in what is called the Upper Room Discourse. In this discourse Jesus was teaching His eleven disciples. Where was the twelfth disciple? Back in JOHN 13 we learn that Judas Iscariot had just left the Last Supper to betray Christ into the hands of sinful men. Judas was the obvious example of one who did not remain in the vine. Judas had abandoned the group of disciples who were following Jesus. Indeed, he became a traitor to the cause. Though Judas had been "in Christ," that is, not saved but in Christ's group of outward followers for three years, he now had left. It is clear that he had borne no fruit, therefore the Father had taken him away.

Later that very evening Jesus would pray in JOHN 17:12, *"While I was with them, I was keeping them in Your name which You have given Me; and I guarded them and not one of them perished but the son of perdition, so that the Scripture would be fulfilled."* Judas departed and perished just like an unfruitful branch. Judas' departure is the context of the vine and branches analogy. It supplies the correct meaning of the parable.

The application of this parable, however, is not to be limited to Judas. Any disciple who starts but does not carry through, who does not join and bear fruit for God, will be thrown away and revealed to be an unbeliever. In John's gospel it says the one who truly believes abides. See JOHN 6:40, 54, and 56. The Lord even explains the intent of the analogy in vv. 7–8. *"If you remain in Me and My words remain in you, ask whatever you wish, and it shall be done for you. By this is My Father glorified that you bear much fruit and so prove to be My disciples."* Faithful abiding produces fruit, and the fruit proves the person is a true disciple of Christ. It proves they have saving faith.

So, Jesus was warning those that would claim to be one of His disciples, that if they abandoned Him and His word, they would be identified by the Father and removed into a judgment of fire. We must always weigh the consequences of turning our back on Christ and walking away. For where we walk will not be to life but to eternal death and destruction.

Peter was faced with this very decision in JOHN 6:66–68: *"As a result of this many of His disciples withdrew and were not walking with Him anymore. So Jesus said to the twelve, 'You do not want to go away also, do you?' Simon Peter answered Him, 'Lord, to whom shall we go? You have the words of eternal life.'"* Do not abandon the One who gives you eternal life! Remain true to Him until the end and you will receive the promises.

Discussion & Application

1. Why is every disciple dependent on Jesus to bear fruit for God?

_____

_____

_____

2. Why is it such treachery to walk away from faith in Jesus Christ? Why does God react to it so harshly?

_____

_____

_____

3. If you worry about not abiding in Christ, what can you ask Jesus to do for you to secure you in the faith?

_____

_____

_____

Key Terms/Phrases

Abide = to remain believing in Jesus; to continue in one's faith and not abandon it for another; to be loyal to Christ

Fruitfulness = the quality of producing good works of faith by remaining in Christ and receiving His life power

Faithful = the state of being true to someone in word and deed

Parable = a figure of speech in short story form to teach a spiritual lesson using familiar settings or events

Further Exploration

John 6:37–39; 10:28–29; 15:1–8; 1 John 2:19–20;
Hebrews 6:4–9; 10:35–39